Guided to the Higher Realms

A Personal Journey of Ascension Through Meditation

Paula Forget

Books of Light Publishing
1810 Larrabee Avenue, Bellingham, WA 98225

For more information, contact:

www.paulaforget.com/inspired
paulaforget1@gmail.com

ISBN: 978-0-692-17400-5
LCCN: 2015947323

Table of Contents

IV – PERIOD OF WAITING & PREPARATION

ILLUSTRATIONS

Preface to the Second Edition

Since the publication of the first edition in 2015, I have received many requests to share my One Minute Power Meditation (1MPM) on line. I added a video link, with detailed instructions, to the 1MPM.

I added a list of illustrations to the table of contents, including illustrations added in Part I, Chapter 3, and Part III, Chapter 8.

I revised Part I, Chapter 3, *Walking through the Door*, to include my early NDE/out-of-body experience. The relevance of their overlapping elements was a strong motivator in stimulating my interest in meditation.

In Part III, Chapter 1 was edited and an additional chapter was added (Chapter 3, *Meditation and Grace*), to improve clarity and flow. A video link was added directing to an interview with the author, titled *The State of Grace*.

The Conclusion was updated to include current observations.

Paula Forget
July 2018

Preface

It is time.

As we walk our path of inner quest, transformation and growth, we strive to reach the inner sanctum of our being and soul. What is this force that touches our heart, that transforms our mind and that opens us up to the Greater Reality? We all dwell within it. All forms of creation dwell within it.

It is time. So much Love is held within each molecule of life. Now is the time to awaken to its power. We are filled with it. We are surrounded by it. We exist because of it.

There was a time when secrets were left unspoken. Now, it is time to reveal, shed light on the higher dimensions of life, to illuminate the way for all. The time is right, the way is clear, leading all to their highest Self. It is time to rejoice in the beauty of the Divine.

Open your heart to the light and the love that permeates all of creation.

It is time for us to purify our hearts. It will point the way to our true destiny. Life's meaning is simple; live your gifts, praise the beauty that is in every molecule of life, follow the highest yearning of your heart.

Namaste

Introduction

I began meditating in the spring of 1998. I was embarking on a spiritual adventure that would unlock the deepest and most profound encounters with the nature of the Divine.

This story demonstrates the spiritual evolution that transformed me, the depth of wisdom gleaned through conversations with enlightened beings and through understanding the nature of the soul. It is an exploration into the nature of consciousness and the soul. The answers to the primordial questions—who am I, why am I here, where did I come from, what happens to me after death— are different for everyone. We each are unique, with our own individual motivations, yet we all share the same pure essence.

Connecting with one's Highest Self is accessible to everyone. What began as a tool to relax and gain inner balance revealed more than I expected. It challenged me to be honest on a deeper level and have the courage to live the depth of my soul.

There are four parts to the book. They delineate the process and stages of development. The four parts are intended to be read in sequence, as the process builds progressively. I use language that can be understood by anyone, explaining some terms familiar in the practice of meditation, as they are presented throughout the book.

There are descriptions of conversations with beings from higher realms. These accounts were written in real time and have been included with very little editing. When they communicate, I experience them on so many levels that it does not all translate in written form. I added explanatory text in brackets to these conversations where needed.

The names of some people and places have been changed to maintain privacy.

Part 1 describes the changes that led to new beginnings in my life, my introduction to the practice of meditation, and meditation's transformative influence physically and spiritually. It describes the higher chakras. I have chosen to refer to the higher levels of consciousness as chakras.

Part 2 continues the ascension process into the higher chakras and communication with higher beings.

Part 3 is a compilation of conversations and teachings from higher beings in preparation to upcoming personal life changes. It also describes the relationship between the Dimensions and chakras. It is presented in the format of a diary, from which it was written.

Part 4 describes the period of waiting, requiring patience and discipline, and then the final arrival of a new life direction.

I

In the Beginning

Chapter 1

The Student Is Ready

These were the first words I heard when I began to write:

"In the Beginning there was the Word . . . The force of the Divine."

This Divine Energy that we are sustained by, this Creative Force that holds Intelligence, this Presence is everywhere, everywhere.

"In the Beginning, there was the Love of God."

What awaited me, I could never have imagined. All had come together like dominoes falling in place. As they say, "when the student is ready, the teacher will arrive."

I was sharing a house in Gainesville, Florida, while working as fine art painter for an art studio. I was introduced by one of my roommates to Charles, who gave meditation classes in his home three nights a week. We would meet in a casual atmosphere and he would give satsang (spiritual talks) and lead us in guided meditations. The first meditation of the evening would often be what he called The One-Minute Power Meditation. It became the foundation of my meditation practice.

During the following two years, I was transformed physically, emotionally, mentally, and spiritually. That is no small transformation.

Chapter 2

Early Foundation

I was born in 1953 in Montreal, Canada, and was adopted into a loving family. I had one brother who was a few years older than me and was a very protective big brother. I enjoyed growing up in this cosmopolitan city. My family was French and I quickly learned to also speak English. My friends were from many cultural backgrounds. I found the exchange rich and stimulating, and I loved being surrounded with a great variety of traditions and religious faiths. I was raised through the Catholic school system by nuns, who taught with strict academic discipline. I had a mostly quiet childhood and was shy and showed a natural aptitude in the arts. I studied ballet and music and spent hours drawing in my room. I was also an avid reader, often reading a book a day. I loved to dive into adventures, mysteries and stories of faraway places. In my teens I read mostly nonfiction and the sciences: physics, the nature of the brain, and human behavior.

As I grew up, I explored my deeper motivations, examining my behavior, and I always had an inner guidance to strive to live an honorable life. I was not new to spiritual development. I have been on the path since my early teens. At the age of twelve, I read Norman Vincent Peale's book *The Power of Positive Thinking* and a few years later studied the hermetic principles of the *Kybalion*, based on the ancient Egyptian Hermetic philosophy.

They both became my standard operating procedure. I proved the principles to myself. I knew that, similar to the universal law "like attracts like," a positive attitude toward life emanated a vibration that guided me to be exactly where I needed to be. I expected it to happen, and so it did. I developed a gut feeling and confidence that life was unfolding for my highest potential and that all I needed to do was to just get out of my own way. The rest would be taken care of. Life is truly magical.

During that time, I also began to have dreams of my future. I would dream of everyday events, nothing special. No earthquakes, no end of the world or cataclysmic events. Then when these events happened, I would recognize them in a flash of recognition, and would remember when I had dreamed of the event. So I started to call them *flashes*.

My first flash was very memorable. One night I dreamed that I was a passenger in a car. I was sitting in the back seat and looking out the window. It felt as though I was in the country, and the car was headed up a wooded tree-lined hill. As I was looking out the window, I suddenly saw a very modern glass house in the shape of a crescent, and I thought, "What is this very modern house doing up here in the middle of nowhere?" The next morning I shared the story with friends in school.

About a month later, I was sitting at a corner soda shop, like the 50's diners that are still popular today, drinking a soda with my school friend Julie. A few minutes later, some of her friends joined us. We all decided to go for a drive, and so off we went. We were casually driving around our area of Montreal and, after a while, took a turn and started going up an exclusive residential area near Mt. Royal. All that was visible were woods all around and an occasional home tucked away. Then as we turned a corner, I recognized the modern house made of glass in the unusual crescent architecture. I realized that in its context, it made sense to see it there. I exclaimed, "I dreamed about that house!"

In the years that followed, the flashes became more frequent. In their most active period, I would dream of the events of the next day, having up to thirty flashes a day. What had been startling at first quickly became a curiosity. I did not understand how they happened, why they happened to me, what caused them to become more frequent, or how to control the process. I found the phenomenon interesting. I began to read books about metaphysics, telepathy and psychic phenomena and the research taking place in the scientific community.

When I graduated from high school, I was determined to understand the nature of these flashes. How could I know the future if it hadn't happened yet? (Or had it?) I wanted to do research on the nature of time. I went to college with the intention of studying the sciences. Would my answer be found in psychology, physics, or biochemistry? There were no concrete sciences that dealt with it. Parapsychology and psychic research were fringe modalities, and I had already read all the studies that I could find in those areas. I did not need to prove to myself that these things existed; what I really wanted to know is *how* did it all work?

In my early twenties, I met a wonderful man from the United States, who was visiting the area. I first found him amusing and stimulating. He had a flexible intellect and loved to travel. We spent hours discussing a wide range of topics from religion to spirituality, science, and culture. He grew up in the South of the United States, and his background was strictly Southern Baptist. When he went to college, he met new people of various backgrounds, and his perspective broadened. Like me, he had a natural curiosity for the world and was open to new experiences. We were a match. We married in the United States and shared twenty years together.

Chapter 3

Walking Through the Door, my NDE

When I arrived in Gainesville in spring of 1998, I was in the middle of many life changes and many new beginnings. I had begun a new life as a single woman after a twenty-year marriage, with a new career, in new surroundings. I felt driven by an inner force, a certainty, and a conviction that the changes were necessary. A veil had been lifted, and now I could see more clearly than ever before. My heart had opened, and I could feel the most subtle nuances of my surroundings. I was now more aware of colors, as vibrations of light, dancing all around me. I could *feel* again and could not deny the Truth that spoke from my heart. Now was the time to act. I had already walked through the first door, and every step forward opened the next. There was no turning back. My eyes were opened.

In early May, I began meditation classes. I remember the first class.

I had just happened to show up as by accident at the teacher's home. I was on my way to a gathering for dinner, along with one of my roommates. He stopped momentarily to drop off some papers he had written about yoga, to be published in the local networking paper for alternative practitioners. The teacher was going to pass them on to the editor. I was waiting in the car. He returned and asked if I would like to attend a meditation class that was just beginning. I thought, "That's different. I'll see what it's all about."

In class, there was a discourse, called satsang, taking place. Satsang was a term used to describe a spiritual teaching. There is usually a moment during the talk when its truth resonates in the heart. That is the special quality of satsang: it speaks to our heart. This satsang was about the Higher Self.

The teacher, Charles, talked about the four parts of the Self: the body, the heart, the mind and the Higher Self. He explained how our minds view the outer world, how our emotions react to our thoughts, and how our bodies, in turn, are affected by our emotions. He spoke at length about the Higher Self. I had always thought in the past that the Higher Self was difficult to connect with. For me, it was as though breaking a spiritual glass ceiling. How do you finally reach it? "Mmmm . . . Interesting topic," I thought to myself.

I later learned to better understand the four parts of the Self. For example, if I felt agitated, I learned to notice where my agitation was originating from. It might be coming from my mind, with active thoughts disturbing my peace. At other times, I might be in the throes of a reactive heart. My feelings would command the flow of my experience, as I held on to my emotions. Or I might feel a physical discomfort or conversely, a good feeling of elation and satisfaction, through physical sensations.

I learned to maintain balance throughout my being by keeping an inner watch and sense of supervision. I learned to recognize that there is a part of me that is always conscious and present. It is the part that is self-aware and watches the inner experiences I was living as I reacted to and interacted with the outer stimulus of my life. I learned to recognize that the higher-resonant Self, balanced and harmonious, was always present and available, if I simply remembered to connect with it. I was discovering that meditation was a means to reintroduce me to my true essence, the primordial Self that is my true Self.

Until I began to resonate and feel the higher vibration of my Higher Self, I was bound to live as the reactive self. The lack of balance had led to disease and ill health. I became very aware that it had brought on my rheumatoid arthritis. After all, it is a disease of the immune system.

Charles began a guided meditation. I had never experienced one, even less had a good idea how to meditate. He began by introducing us to the One-Minute Power Meditation.[1] It would actually last about two to five minutes, depending on how quickly it was done. He had us observe our bodies, then our emotional heart centers, followed by our minds and their current levels of activity. Then he gently guided us out of our bodies to a ball of light. He was comforting and comfortable in his guidance and I felt no fear. He connected us with the light's

---

1   A video introduction to the One Minute Power Meditation is available at www.paulaforget.com/inspired.

The One Minute Power Meditation

power called Source. It was as though we were connecting with the power of the divine. I recognized a familiar quality in this Source. (It brought back to me the memory of an event I had had over 20 years earlier. I will share more in a moment.) I also felt as though there was a magnetic beam of light creating a connection between it and me.

Then the feeling was directed down as a beam of light through the top of my head to my heart center. I was fused with this beam emanating from Source. My heart felt calm, serene, and not emotional. I noticed I could still feel the connection later in the evening when I recalled the meditation.

Charles spoke about spirituality from the knowledge of one who has experienced life, has grown through spiritual practice and discipline, and has reached a significant level of development. I recognized that his understanding went beyond book learning, and it resonated with me.

Illustration: The One Minute Power Meditation

This first meditation brought back to me a familiar feeling. When I was 19 years old, I had an out-of-body experience— an event that changed my view of life.

At that time, I had already been researching the nature of the mind and consciousness for many years, because of my precognitive dreams. For me, it was a fertile time of inquiry. I read studies conducted by Dr. Rhine at Duke University, along with other studies taking place in Europe and the Soviet Union. Also during those years, I learned about the Eastern religious teachings that the Beatles brought to the West, after visiting the Maharishi Mahesh Yogi in India, who taught them Transcendental Meditation as a tool to bring peace of mind.

Then in the early '70s I read about the ceremonial use of psychoactive substances, as used by indigenous people for millennia, as a doorway to religious experience. Their traditions seemed foreign to me and I wondered what insights they gained from the practice. I also studied the Hindu and Buddhist views of consciousness and reincarnation. While my understanding was superficial and I did not pursue meditation at that time, my research provided me with enough familiarity that I thought I might delve deeper into the Eastern wisdoms some day. After all, I was only a teenager and had other more active interests.

One afternoon, I was visiting a friend who shared an interest in telepathy, spirituality, and mysticism. He had an extensive library of fascinating books that I would read for hours. On this afternoon, I was sitting at a table drawing and playing with crayons. He gave me a substance that he said had the potential to expand my awareness. I took it and did not feel anything at first. Then I heard a swishing sound in my ears and saw a tunnel begin to form in the corner of the room. It was only in my peripheral view and I ignored it, engrossed in my drawing. After a few moments, I noticed that the tunnel had grown larger and was swirling. I stopped to watch it, wondering what it was. The next moment, I was pulled in and being sucked up the tunnel!

I started to wonder if it was the tunnel that is often described by people who have near-death experiences. I was not happy: I didn't want to go. I had left my body and had no control over the experience. I began to resist, as I was quickly being carried upward. I felt as though I was in the center of a tornado. The more I fought, the more I was hitting the sides of the tunnel. It was becoming a rough ride. So, realizing that I could not control what was happening, I finally gave up and surrendered to the force that was pulling me upward, which made everything feel much smoother. The current gradually began to slow and eventually stopped.

I looked around and found myself in a dimly lit place. It was dark but not black. There was nothing there. I was there alone. Then I realized something that I had never experienced before. This place had no time or space. I felt as though my spirit was standing in eternity and infinity. Moreover, I was filled with the most absolute feeling of peace and contentment that I had ever known. I knew I could feel this way forever and ever.

I enjoyed the "moment," although there was no time, and after a "while," I started to wonder what had happened to my body that I had left sitting in the chair at the table. Did I die? Was I in a coma? I started thinking about my parents and how devastated they would be to see me gone. I had visions of my friend whose home I was visiting. If I was found dead or in a coma, he would have to deal with an awful situation.

After another "while," I decided to come back. Somehow I knew I belonged in my life on earth. But how was I going to do that? I felt as though what had happened to me was an accident. Now I was in a place that was so different —eternal, and never-changing. I had even lost the ability to think with words! I was pure consciousness. With my knowledge of science and metaphysics, I started to think (without words) that time and space was the element that differed between where I was and the earth. Perhaps if I could imagine the feeling of time and space, it would bring me back? So with great effort, I tried to remember words, and finally said: "Don't I have to be somewhere, sometime?" IMMEDIATELY I was back sitting in my chair, by the desk. I raised my head and opened my eyes. I was back.

After that experience, I never thought the same way about death again. The timeless sense of peace and contentment I had felt was sublime. I knew that my spirit was eternal and that the transition was as easy as walking from one room to another. Whenever my time came, I would welcome it.

When I had my first meditation at Charles's class and went up to Source, I found myself in the same place I had experienced 20 years earlier, experiencing the same feelings of timelessness, peace, and contentment. I exclaimed to myself: "I've been here before!" This realization made me want to learn more about meditation, and I decided to return for the next class.

At the next meeting, Charles spoke about our chakras and our etheric bodies. I was familiar with the concepts, but had no real experience of my chakras. I was just beginning to feel my heart! I was familiar with a subtle etheric body though, having done research into Kirlean photography, a technique for photographing people's auras, during my twenties. My husband and I had done a study tracking the female menstrual cycle by taking a Kirlean photo of each participant at the same time every day over a period of three months. We were able to observe the cyclical pattern reflected in participants' energetic fields. In my teen years, I had also noticed that I could sense the energetic field of a plant by placing my hand a few inches above it and noticing a faint magnetic pressure in the air. I noticed how it responded to my presence when its field grew larger. I practiced with different varieties of plants sensing how they felt; some had a soft presence, and others might emit a strong field.

During the meditation session, I discovered that my energetic field was composed of many etheric bodies. I noticed their different densities. Yes, they had a finer quality about them. (I read a book many years later, *Hands of Light*, by Barbara Brennan, that described them well.) We did more exercises connecting us with our Source and bringing down the energy into our bodies, activating our chakras and this time, radiating the pure energy outward. I really enjoyed the experience.

Later that evening, I decided to plan my own personal meditation time. I realized that I needed to sort out and align the four parts of my Self: the physical, emotional, mental, and spiritual. Wow! That was a huge Ah-ha moment! I had never viewed it that way, but it was clear that the four parts were interrelated. What had seemed an intriguing topic at first was becoming a new path of inner exploration.

I was confident about my life choices at this time, but it was still a difficult period of change. I was emotionally grieving the breakup of my marriage, and I was challenged by the adjustments required in my new life. The reduced income and career change made me fearful that I would not be able to earn enough to cover my living expenses. I had cut back to the bare minimum and still had to take on a second, and sometimes third, job to make ends meet. I could see that the rheumatoid arthritis that I'd had for four years now was causing a decline in my physical strength and flexibility. I was in constant pain. My hands had limited mobility due to the inflammation, and the joint pain had spread to my elbows, shoulders, knees, ankles, and feet. I thought my life was over! Not really, but my future prospects did not look good. I would try to brush those thoughts aside, but because of the constant pain, they were still in the back of my mind.

This meditation time would help me face those challenges. I would have to really learn to be aware of my body, open myself to the true feelings in my heart, and also observe the thought patterns of my mind. This would require work.

Illustration: The Four Parts of the Self

4 Parts of the Self

Chapter 4

I Am as a Roaring Flame

I remember his words: "See how high you can go."

I continued going to class. I learned to tune in with my Higher Self. It was a calmer and wiser Self and had a gentle quality about it. I realized that its special quality had a higher, more evolved perspective, and that it resonated with the fine and pure vibration found in the ball of light, the light from Source. During the One-Minute Power Meditation, I would systematically take a personal assessment of my inner state of being. I would examine my body, heart, and mind and then connect with a beautiful ball of light located high above the top of my head. I learned that it was actually located in one of the higher chakras. Within the ball of light, I would experience absolute peace, love, and contentment, where all time stopped and I felt infinite. What a blissful state! I also learned that I could bring the feelings back with me into my physical body and, in time, feel them whenever I wanted to. Charles suggested that we do the One-Minute Power Meditation five times a day. For many people, it was easier to do five deep One-Minute Power Meditations and easier to commit to, than to plan time for a long meditation. Most people found it daunting to sit down and consistently meditate for twenty to thirty minutes each day. They didn't have time, they were too busy, and it was too difficult to focus with all the busyness in their lives. On the other hand, to focus on the One-Minute Power Meditation was quick. It covered all the parts of the Self, was refreshing, provided deep relaxation, and reconnected us with the best parts of our Selves. Afterwards, we resumed our life activities with renewed energy.

I realized that it was easy for me to meditate. Being a natural artist, I had spent hours as a child focusing on drawing, coloring books, playing with clay, and reading. So I could easily hold my focus during meditation.

In June we did a special meditation to commemorate the Wesak Festival, a Hindu tradition. On this day, we are given a view of the next twelve months and the path of our spiritual development.

The session began with the One-Minute Power Meditation. I went into the ball of light and felt myself radiating light in all directions. As I looked out into infinity, I saw other balls of light and felt sweetness, love, and innocence radiating everywhere. I sensed the year pass by in front of me very quickly and leave me with peace in my heart.

As I sat in the blissful state of my Higher Self, Charles guided us higher still. I continued rising upward, and I thought of repeating the process, rising up through the top of my head and, experiencing a finer and more subtle awareness of myself, as a new Higher Self. I repeated the process two more times, rising from my Higher Self, to *its* Higher Self, and I then felt myself become as a roaring flame, filled with power: my heart was exalted. Charles then said, "Who are you in that place?"

This flame felt so powerful that I exclaimed to myself, "I am as a roaring flame!" I brought this feeling of power back with me, back down through the layers of my Higher Selves, back into my physical body. I thought to myself, "Its power gives me strength," and my heart felt, "All of life is Grace and Beauty and Understanding."

I still do not know how I knew to continue rising above my Higher Self and do that exercise. Over the years, I have often noticed that I spontaneously know what to do.

Illustration: Rising Up

Rising up

Chapter 5
Feel Everything

The next weeks and months became a very active period of self-discovery. I was practicing the One-Minute Power Meditation five times a day, and in the evening would make time for longer meditations, exploring more deeply the four parts of my Self. I was experiencing a period of spiritual acceleration. I gained quick insights on the qualities of the etheric world. I noticed myself becoming more familiar with my Higher Selves. Every time I would ascend to a higher level, the quality of my state of consciousness would become even more serene and clear, as if it were the smooth surface of a pool of water. I became aware of the special qualities of the higher chakras in the same way as those of my light bodies. I learned that I could use the chakras vibrations to perform healings on my physical body.

I also realized that I could feel inside people's hearts, more than just compassion or empathy, it was a *knowing*, a fullness of understanding. I could now feel people's thoughts and emotions, as real, physical vibrations. I practiced speaking directly to people's Higher Selves. I realized that speaking this way is our natural state.

I knew that I had become numb over the years. I had *settled*— compromised, agreed to conform to the expectations of my family, my job, society. I had often thought, "I don't know if I really like this, but I guess it's OK." I had been taught to be quiet and agreeable and not make waves. I was Miss Congeniality. Part of me was a naturally happy and cheerful person, yet another part felt unheard, hurt, fearful and timid. I had developed the habit of not feeling my true feelings. They were not permitted to be heard or expressed. So much had been colored by others' preferences. I had become the personality that everyone wanted to see. I had tried to be all things to all people.

When I began my new life as a single woman again, I was determined to look at myself honestly. I wanted to feel fully again. I wanted to feel everything. No more walls, no more excuses or rationalizations. It was such a painful and soul-searching time of personal honesty. My heart had been opened and now I could feel the true nature of the world around me.

To be able to effectively meditate, it was important for me to feel with an open heart. With meditation I was given a way to truly examine the state of my physical body, the concerns of my heart, and the quality of my thoughts. I had never truly noticed how interrelated they were. A simple emotional feeling could bring on a stream of thought patterns, followed by a physiological response throughout my body.

I had been taught the One-Minute Power Meditation, a deceptively simple exercise, easy to learn, yet more engaging than I had at first expected. I then found myself making time for longer meditations. When I first began this meditation practice, I would spend reflective time examining my true feelings and reviewing past events of my life. I would examine my beliefs, how I had arrived at them, the soundness of their precepts, and how they had directed the course of my decisions. I would notice my reactions, emotionally and physically: my body would tense up, my muscles would stiffen, I would feel waves of emotion come over me. At last, I wanted to *feel everything*! Then, I let them all go. What a relief it was. It was work. It was a necessary process.

Chapter 6

My House, My Purpose

On occasion, Charles would channel a Guide, a spiritual being who acts as a teacher and often guides us to the higher realms, to lead the meditation. The guide would direct us to our higher chakras and allow us to experience the subtle dimensions of our Selves. Charles was a proficient channel and on this day, a new guide to this group introduced himself as Bartholomew. I recognized him as an advanced spirit by the quality of his demeanor.

He had us visualize a vibrant green field with short grass. Then, he had us stand there in our light bodies and visualize a building forty to fifty feet ahead of us. This would be our house where we could go to find answers to our questions.

I walked through the green meadow over to my house. My house was a round, white dome. It had no doors, only an open archway. I saw Bartholomew to my right. To me, he looked a little like Moses in the Bible, with a long white beard, but strong, virile and wise. I looked at him spiritually, my spirit to his spirit, and although I had never met him, I recognized the Knowledge he held in him and he recognized it in me. We each had a huge smile and were exhilarated by it. "The light that we both share is so joyous," I thought. I know that my whole face lit up. I felt elated.

Bartholomew said, "Go into the house and enter into the room through the door that your third eye is guiding you to." I looked inside and could see that the interior had a circular wall, like a silo, with white doors, but only on the ground floor. I experienced the house as being infinite, as having levels going upward, and I was aware of many invisible rooms. It felt very vast, reaching up and outwards, although still contained within its circular perimeter. It had no roof.

Bartholomew said, "Go to the room that has the answer you seek. You will naturally, effortlessly be drawn to the room you need to go to." I felt myself float inside a room and felt myself ask the question, "What am I supposed to do?"

I *felt* the answer, in all sweetness and gentleness, come over me as a soft ripple that I could see, almost a pink/white ripple flowing to and through me. And within my being, I *knew* the answer as it said, "Show the Beauty."

The words *Show the Beauty* carried with them a fuller meaning beyond the simple, pretty, esthetically pleasing quality of the world. I sensed within those words the beauty of love, the beauty of the miracle of life, the beauty of the simplest task, the beauty of suffering and courage, dedication and devotion, compassion, despair and grace. The Beauty of Divine Expression.

Yes, I recognized that it is my gift, that I see the Beauty, that my heart, my soul, my essence, is totally immersed in the Joy and Beauty of the entire universe. It was so obvious. Why did I not see it before? It is the essence of my being. *I had already been doing it my whole life.* It didn't matter *what* I did, it was *how* I did it that expressed my essence. Show the Beauty. It was so simple.

Yes, I could see it. My nickname had been, over and over again, Paula Sunshine. I was always dancing in the Beauty of life. That is the side of me that I had been encouraged to express. Now I would develop a fuller expression of myself.

There was no great plan or goal to reach. Just being my Self was enough. I later realized that is all each of us is called upon to do. Expressing our true essence is our greatest form of expression.

Chapter 7

Vibrational Tone & Resonance

During meditation I learned to notice the feelings projected by the beings that I encountered. I would feel them as a vibration, a quality of intention that carried information about the beings. I called this feeling a vibrational tone. The tone is felt and has resonance. I later noticed that places and objects also carried signature feelings, residual feelings imprinted from their owners. When I meditated, I was aware of the importance of setting a good vibrational tone that would attract beings of similar quality.

My longer meditations followed the well-defined structure of the One-Minute Power Meditation. They proceeded in an orderly fashion, as I began each session by establishing a sacred space, environment, and tone. I would take a personal inventory of my physical, emotional, and mental states of being and then notice the quality of my spiritual vibration.

Sometimes I would meditate with a specific goal or spiritual task, such as healing, reflecting deeply on the quality of my heart, or benefiting others. Other times I would simply rest my attention on the quality of the eternal moment. When completing the meditation session, I would then bring my attention back to my surroundings, back to my physical body—feel the sensation of my arms, hands, legs and feet. I would express gratitude for the Love and Grace received during the session. I would always end by savoring the Beauty of the eternal moment.

I returned several times again to my house. There would usually be a kind being there to greet me when I arrived.

One time I arrived at the green meadow, then met Bartholomew at the entrance to my house. He directed me inside to the main room and I stood there and looked up to the infinite sky. I began to fly upward in the silo-like central area of my house. I flew like a bird, gliding through and around the invisible rooms and levels. I could see the blue sky above and my whole being felt calm and peaceful.

Then I unexpectedly caught glimpses of etheric beings, soaring past me, and I felt their presence and their calm, light joy, in my heart, a sense of lightness that was new to me. I realized that the *lightness* of their souls is what is captured in the paintings of angels. The wings in the paintings are figurative wings that represent their feelings of lightness and freedom. The deep calm and peace I felt in my heart, soul, and whole being was the angelic quality I recognized in them. There was a delicacy and lightness about it all. I understood what was *meant* by angels now.

I left my house, passed Bartholomew at the entrance, went back to the green meadow, and then back to my body in an orderly fashion.

On another occasion when I visited my house, I had a different kind of surprising encounter. It was the first time I had experienced a physical channeling.

I decided to go to my house and be open to experiencing new knowledge. I rose to my Higher Self then up to the realm where my house is. I went to the grassy area, where I felt the sun shining on me and felt the joy of being there. Then I went to the doorway and was greeted by Bartholomew. I entered, stopped, and instinctively sat down and began to meditate, opening myself to impressions.

I started to feel and see a very dense energy twisting down through the top of my head. I twisted with it and became saturated with its density. It then began to take on human form. I especially felt its face. "An unpleasant personality," I thought, "Not light and fun like me!" My face began to reflect its personality, my lower lip curling out. The person was very heavy—felt like 300 pounds. I felt very heavy, my physical body weighed down to the bed I was sitting on.

I began to think, "I hope this person will not be a regular visitor. He is not very pleasant (and fun). I don't care what he knows." I began to feel tired, so I requested that it end. I felt him begin to lift away, and I gradually became myself again. I asked Bartholomew to help me regain my composure. Then I proceeded back to the grassy area and back down to my body sitting on the bed.

Little did I know on that day that "the 300 Pounder" would become my serious "no-nonsense" teacher for years to come and I would learn more about his role in my life. The teachings I would receive were not to be taken lightly. He had wanted to make a strong first impression and indeed he did.

On August 20, 1998, was held the World Wide Meditation Day promoting global harmony. (It was similar to an event that now takes place every year during the International Day of Peace in September). I sat in meditation, connected with the collective presence of all those who were participating in the event and felt their collective vibrational tone. I was now able to differentiate the vibrational signature of individuals, groups and places. My senses were developing as I was accessing new dimensions of life.

In addition to learning how to differentiate vibrational signatures and developing my senses, I was learning to sustain my focus for longer periods of time. Because of this, I loved to perform distance healings for friends, at times visiting up to three people in one sitting. It was work, and I often asked for help from higher dimensional healers. I learned much by watching them. I also asked for help in treating the rheumatoid arthritis in my body.

One day during class, Charles told us we would be meditating along with a group of advanced guides and masters for the next couple of months. He directed us to go up to the realm where the group was sitting in a circle. I then saw a dim circle, as if it was night time, like the circle of a powwow. The masters were sitting in the circle and I could *feel* their presence and their Wisdom and Knowledge.

Charles said to ask the elders for our assignment for meditation. I then saw nature, beautiful and green, vibrant, glowing, and twinkling with light. I could feel the life in it on a cellular level. I then looked down at all the nature on Earth and felt its life, glowing in its splendor.

Next we went up to where the ball of light was and imagined ourselves *being* the ball of light and also *seeing* ourselves as the ball of light at the same time. Finally, we imagined ourselves focusing into ourselves and i*mploding*, and then at that moment *exploding outward* into a million billion lights of all the colors of the universe—*feeling* them all, and *being* them all. I realized that I could have the consciousness of an entire galaxy. I felt serious at first and then light and happy.

I brought this feeling back to the meditation circle, where again I saw the beautiful light green of nature. The colors were vibrating in harmony, and I thought, "Yes, this is something I can do, to meditate on nature, and I'll enjoy doing it too." Then I came back in an orderly manner.

In the following days and weeks, I visited the powwow circle and saw the elders there sitting inside the circle, setting the vibrational tone. There would be others along the outer circle, also meditating, and the participants would change, sometimes more people, sometimes only a few. Everyone was very serious and focused. I noticed that they were different from me. I am light and happy. But still, I applied myself and did my assigned exercise of meditating on nature.

During the summer, a group of Tibetan monks came to Gainesville for an entire week. They performed their traditional music and dances at the Fine Arts Center. Over several days, they created a sand mandala at the public library downtown. I went to watch them one afternoon and was surprised to notice that the mandala was a 3-D representation of the intricate diagrams I had seen in photographic prints. The details appeared as individual objects of colored sand, created with exquisite precision. At the end of the week, they swept up the magnificent creation, and during a ceremony, the sand was released into a nearby stream, symbolizing life's impermanence.

The group was composed of several older monks, no doubt teachers who fled from the ancient monasteries in Tibet to escape the Chinese invasion in the 1950s. Along the older monks were also younger monks, who lived with the older monks in India, where new monasteries were now their homeland.

They gave several talks during their stay. The older monks gave their teachings in their traditional tongue and the younger monks would translate for us into English.

I attended one of the talks. The monks began the meeting with their deep-throated chanting. They are able to resonate several notes simultaneously, which creates a unique sound. The traditional chants represent a lineage that has been passed on through generations. The chants were followed by a discourse given by one of the eldest monks.

During the main talk, three other very elderly monks sat quietly, meditating the entire time. As I listened to the lesson, I became aware that the meditating monks were projecting pictures of their homeland into the room, on a subtle level of consciousness, to everyone's Higher Self. There were two conversations going on! I saw the beautiful mountains and valleys of their homeland. They also projected uplifting, pure intentions in the forms of feelings. They needed no words to communicate with us.

After the talk, there was a question and answer period on the principles and practice of Buddhism. I finally felt that it was time for me to ask a question that had been on my mind all evening: "What can I or anyone do to help to make it possible for them to regain their homeland?" I felt powerless to help this peaceful nation that was having their culture destroyed, and the images projected throughout the evening only fueled my feeling of inadequacy. The monk thanked me for asking the question and said, "Put pressure on the United States government to speak to China on our behalf." This last question ended the evening.

The day before the group left, they conducted the Medicine Buddha Initiation in a small room that held about seventy-five people. It was a guided meditation that originated above the top of the head. We were asked to visualize seven Buddhas stacked above our head, (like seven chakras). Each had a specific character and color. We then moved down each Buddha, asking him to join us, accumulating energy from each one along the way. I finally entered my physical body, through the top of my head, as we were told to imagine ourselves now as a crystal of pure healing light, radiating healing power outward onto the world.

I felt totally saturated by this amazing healing energy in my body. I went home and straight to sleep. Got up the next morning and went to work. Afterwards, I came back home to sleep some more. I did that for three days. That was quite an initiation!

I started to practice the vibrational tones in public places. I had fun, for instance, going to the grocery store and quietly emanating a "tonal field of light" around me. I would notice how people would instinctively turn around to see where it was coming from. It's interesting how we can sense things on a subtle level. Haven't we all noticed when someone is watching us, and we turn around to see who it is? Or we can sense the mood of people in line at a store and know if they are happy, sad, or preoccupied, or perhaps angry or impatient. It is more than just body language. We feel the mood of a place when we walk into a doctor's waiting room or at a gathering of strangers attending a lecture. A single person can walk in and affect the entire tone by his presence.

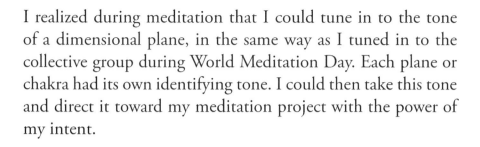

I realized during meditation that I could tune in to the tone of a dimensional plane, in the same way as I tuned in to the collective group during World Meditation Day. Each plane or chakra had its own identifying tone. I could then take this tone and direct it toward my meditation project with the power of my intent.

I also noticed in my meditations now that when I vibrated my energy tone, it was a way to make my presence felt in the realms. It was a way of stating that I had arrived. I also enjoyed vibrating my tone along with the realm, in harmony with its character, strengthening its field. It was really interesting how I could feel so calm and peaceful and could be glowing power at the same time. This activity unified me with the realm. It was Grace to be able to experience it. There was always a sense that the realms are an expression of Divine creation. I continue to be humbled by it.

II

Growth & Ascension

Chapter 1

The Meditator-for-Hire

I began to learn more about the 300 Pounder. During meditation, I channeled him for the second time. He was definitely no-nonsense and serious. That was when I realized that he is, as I would call him, a "meditator-for-hire." He was very good at meditating, an expert. He displayed a lot of power in his focusing ability.

The 300 Pounder had a mastery of handling vibrational tones and directing them with power. It was his assignment to practice his talent and teach it to others. I thought: "He is a meditator-for-hire in the realm. How about that!"

I had no way of knowing at this time that he would, in fact, hold a much greater role in my development. He was my master teacher. In the same way that we might play a role in our own families, as a brother, sister, or parent, his role was to watch over my development, as a parent would. I had been assigned to him, for him to oversee my development. I also came to realize much later that we each have a purpose to serve and uplift the Divine Collective.

He began to teach me higher techniques of meditation and healing. He also directed other teachers, subordinate to him, to assist me from time to time with their individual expertise.

I learned that all our teachers, guides, and helpers on the other side have their own jobs/assignments, which they have agreed to do for their own continued spiritual growth.

Chapter 2

The Eleventh & Twelfth Chakras

I continued to practice ascending to the next levels. By September, I tried to rise to the eleventh chakra, the next level beyond the white ball of light that I occupied during the One-Minute Power Meditation. I noticed that the level felt like glass, like water, a very smooth, calm and timeless feeling. I could easily look *down* to the ball of light. I would also look outward all around me, and it appeared very smooth with colored streaks, like a sunset. I also noticed that my light body was not as clear or clean as it could be to better appreciate the realm. I needed to refine myself more, to become purer. I did not feel *dirty*, just not quite as *compatible* with the realm. I was missing out on some of the experience. I need to ask how to make my light body *finer*.

The next day I went to the twelfth chakra. It felt as though it was somewhat connected to the eleventh chakra. As I was in the eleventh chakra, I rose above my light body, through the top of its head. I looked up and immediately felt myself in a state of suspended animation, as at the moment of realization of orgasm. I felt myself falling back a little: it was overwhelming, intense and also calm at the same time. It was ecstatic, beyond words or emotions—it felt *absolute*. A knowing and realization. I felt as though nothing else existed: it was timeless and infinite.

The meditation lasted thirty minutes. I felt stunned and laid there thinking about it after. So I decided to try to reconnect with it quickly, to recapture the feeling. I went back up to the realm, and there were people waiting for me there, many people. I felt very altered and light. They looked transparent and I felt very calm. I came back in my regular, orderly manner. I was grateful for the possibility to have been there and thanked my guides.

The feelings lingered with me for quite some time afterwards. Yes, I remembered Charles's words again, "See how high you can go," and I was very grateful for the encouragement I had received in the past.

The next day, I think I was still emotionally saturated. I felt like crying. I was struck by the overwhelming realization of the Beauty of Creation, the marvel of it all and how it is expressed on Earth.

Chapter 3
Geography of the Higher Chakras

I had noticed the way the eighth to the twelfth chakras felt. They each had a character and feeling of their own.

The eighth chakra is the level where your subtle bodies, those that are connected to your physical body, sense from. Here is where you experience ESP, dreams, past lives, ghosts, spirits that have not moved on from their lives on Earth by their own choice for various reasons, and lost souls.

The ninth chakra is the level where souls that have been reborn after their lives on Earth, but are not incarnated, assist, serve and guide us. They had moved on to the tenth chakra after death, where they reviewed their lives and decided that they could best grow from that point on by providing service through the ninth chakra. They still carry a lot of the previous identity that they had on Earth and are still overcoming some of their weaknesses. These souls are experiencing a period of redemption as a means to continue their path of growth. The ninth chakra also is occupied by beings from higher realms, as their service requires. They can more easily be sensed by us through this chakra.

The tenth chakra is the level where souls who are transitioning from life on Earth to the afterlife go. It is still concerned with affairs of the Earth. This is where a life review takes place, where advanced beings assist the soul in deciding the next course of action. From here, some souls move up to higher realms, and some choose to go back to the ninth chakra or Earth. The tenth chakra is where the soul rejoins deceased family and friends. This level is vast and encompasses higher realms. This level is what has been described as heaven; here and above reside dimensional hierarchies: here and above are schools of higher learning, where souls are educated in the esoteric spiritual sciences, inner purification, and continued ascension. It also includes other worlds that resonate on the same level.

The eleventh chakra is the level where souls continues to lose density and become more and more subtle, until they finally lose all physicality and are pure consciousness. In this level exists other worlds, as well as beings that have progressively higher wisdom and creative ability (power). Beings that are not associated with Earth matters exist in this level.

The twelfth chakra and above are the levels of pure consciousness, where beings exist in their pure form, with no physicality. Here, they can still create worlds, and as they move up even higher, they exist beyond individuality.

Illustration: Geography of the Higher Chakras

The 8th and 9th chakras are closely related to Earth experience. They can be perceived at times, to a greater and lesser degree, within our conscious and unconscious levels of awareness. The

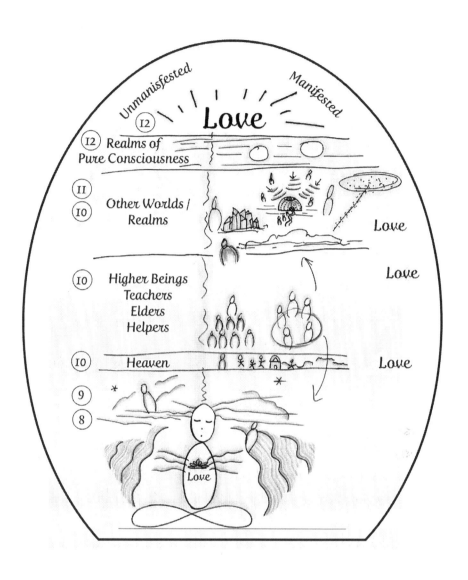

Geography of the Higher Chakras

10th Chakra includes Heaven, spiritual teachers, hierarchies of beings and other worlds and realms of life. We begin to experience timelessness and become aware of the vastness of infinity. The 11th chakra is where there are infinite worlds, some with no connection to the Earth, with infinite levels of density and expressions of higher consciousness. The 12th chakra is occupied by beings of pure consciousness that have no physicality, and beyond is simply the Pure Essence, manifested and unmanifested.

The ability to merge with Divine consciousness is present in all the chakras. During the One-Minute Power Meditation, the ball of light is your connection with the Divine Source. The experience of it deepens as we gain spiritual purity and lose density.

I decided to do an exercise that would focus on the various chakras.

I began the self-guided meditation. Instead of looking for visual cues in my mind's eye, I identified where I was by the characteristic feeling of the realm or chakra. I first went to the powwow (9th chakra), where the others were busy meditating. It felt very happy there on that day, and I was aware that everyone was in great form and upbeat. I did my homework of meditating on the Earth and nature. This time I focused on adjusting and correcting the field of life that surrounds every life-form and then unifying it so that there were no gaps between life-forms. I unified their fields, leaving them connected in their life forces. The powwow circle felt so great that I didn't want to leave, but I still had places to go and things to do, so I left.

I went up to the tenth chakra of light and felt the special character of its tone. Then I went up to the eleventh chakra and could feel the calm and electric feeling there. Finally, I slipped up to the twelfth chakra—into its absolute, timeless, and infinite state. I had trouble concentrating due to its mindless (no thought) nature and decided to return.

I did the same exercise as was done during the Tibetan meditation and brought back the feeling from the realms one into the other, each in turn, back into my seventh and sixth chakras. I then joined the feelings of the lower five chakras up to the sixth. It was a good meditation, and I learned to feel the tones of each realm and chakra.

Later on, I came to realize that there are an infinite number of realms beyond the familiar twelve chakras, and also more than one form of Absolute Timelessness. I wondered, what is this feeling that is beyond Love? What are these realizations that are beyond Grace? I reflected on the nature of the Divine and wrote a poem:

The Divine

The Divine is Eternal and Infinite, never created, never ending.
It holds all of potentiality and existence.
It is the "soup" that sustains and maintains cohesion.
It is the fabric of the universe. This is its nature and life force.
It maintains and supports.
It needs nothing and hears everything. It senses all the hopes, dreams, joy and pain.
It is the giver of Grace.
It is the cradle and the void.

Chapter 4

Fear, Insecurity & Courage

By December, I realized that I had worked on myself for so many years, (my whole life!), and that at this stage in my life I had few things that were major issues for me. In particular, I realized that all that was left, the hurdles I had to face now, were the ones I had put off as the toughest to face. They were my fears and insecurities. I had to face them now to be able to grow. It was time to *act*. There was no other thing left to do.

The greater the resistance inside me, the greater the growth I would derive from it. However, on my side, was the Love, the Source of Wisdom, the guidance, and the connection with the flow and synchronicity. I knew who I was, what my purpose was, and I had Love in my heart.

I was so grateful for these blessings.

In class, Charles stressed the importance of sincerity and Truth in relating with people. To communicate Truth is not a question of analysis and intellect. It is a matter of expressing one's essence— the total makeup of one's spiritual, emotional, and physical being— in a sincere and genuine way. That is

Truth. Truth is a *real, living* thing, not a concept out there. Truth is about *now*, reality in the present.

I told Charles I would like him to talk about courage sometime.

In class I asked a channeled being, how I could find courage to overcome my fears and insecurities. He said that I had been *festering*, like picking on an old scab and keeping it from healing. He said that the child in me was reacting from a memory of something that occurred when I was six years old. He recommended that I meditate and regress back to the event and recall how it felt and how I related with courage and fear from the event. I would understand . . .

Later that evening, I meditated and saw myself as six years old. Such a pure and beautiful child, a sensitive child. I could also see myself looking out into the world with such a delicate disposition, such a purity of spirit. When I compared that to myself now, I felt rough, like sandpaper. My intent was like rough sandpaper, as though stuff was attached to my being and needed to be sloughed off, like dead skin. That was what I was working on clearing now but could not uncover any specific event.

I later spoke to my older brother and asked him if he remembered anything important that happened to me when I was six years old. He told me that I had been beat up by neighborhood boys. They pulled large chunks of my hair, although they did not hurt me seriously. But everyone, my parents and my brother, were very upset by it and a big deal was made of it.

A few years later, during meditation, I was given more insight on this event. I revisited the encounter and saw myself as the six year old walking down the sidewalk a few houses away from my home. I was approached by a gang of young boys a few years older than me. One of the boys decided to begin bullying me, taking advantage of my young age and gentle demeanor. He was pushing me and being rough, and as I was trying to fight back, he used even more force. I was confused. I didn't understand why he was behaving this way, and I could not defend myself from him. He was older, bigger, and stronger than me. He appeared superior to me in every way, and I felt powerless. Any defense on my part was futile, and I wondered what would happen next. I felt hurt, overwhelmed, alone, and afraid. He quickly stopped—I did not know why—and led his friends to continue on down the sidewalk. Relieved, I went home, still confused by the event.

During the meditation, I saw my Higher Self standing behind the boy, examining the scene and his motives for the aggression. I saw his thoughts and felt his feelings. He was reacting to a previous incident that had occurred in his home. His father was abusive, and the boy felt powerless to do anything about it. He was emotionally hurt and crushed by the situation. His intention during the attack was not to hurt me specifically, but only to regain his sense of power. He knew that I could not defend myself from him. He was older, bigger, and stronger than me, like his father was to him. He expressed his rage and frustration on me. He impressed his friends with this false display of authority, which added to his renewed confidence. With this new insight, I felt compassion for him and his pain and wished I could understand other people's misdeeds in this way also.

Afterwards I realized that I have a lot of inner strength and courage and my fears are all imaginary. I had undertaken drastic lifestyle changes and had faith in the course my path was taking.

During class we also talked about the feeling of being tested. When you are being tested:

- You know what you should do.
- You must see it to its completion to know the outcome.
- You are being given an opportunity to learn—the Grace is to be aware of the test.

I felt as though my new life path was a test. I knew that I had to experience these changes. I knew that the road might not be easy, and that there were many unknowns ahead of me. I also knew that the outcome would reveal a great gift.

Charles often said, "The bigger the lions at the gate, the greater the treasure behind it." The lions were my fears, obstacles, or struggles. The treasure was still to be revealed.

Chapter 5
The Blue Chair

At times, Charles would perform what he called "an activation." He would select someone in the class to come and sit in a plain, blue chair that was in the room. He would balance their chakras and send healing energy where needed.

On one occasion, I was invited to sit in the chair. First, he asked me to relax. I must have felt a little nervous. He told me to relax my solar plexus chakra, releasing all fears. I did and sat patiently waiting for his instructions. He said to focus my attention on the place nine feet above the top of my head. I felt very relaxed, in a passive way, as though waiting for something.

I saw two guides approaching me, one on each side of me, coming from behind me. To my left was the guide of Healing, the one to ask for assistance for my health needs. Then my focus moved to the guide approaching on my right. I could feel that he was Love, warm and very friendly and happy. The closer he came to me, the stronger his presence felt, until he finally felt as a warm blanket wrapping itself around my shoulders and my arms. The feeling went right down through my body, my solar plexus, and was so comforting, as though I could never be alone again. I would never feel the feeling of hopeless solitude again because I was wrapped in the comfort of Love.

Charles said to reach out to the other two people in the room and fill them with the energy of the Love. I wrapped them both up with it, as though with a blanket of Love.

The guides then raised my vibrational level and I could feel it throughout my body. They had me access the white light and bring it back down into myself. (I usually would have flown up to it instead, but did not because it would not have been polite to leave the two guides who were there to see me!) I brought the white light into my physical body and could feel myself glow.

I noticed that I felt even better than I felt normally now these days, and I had been feeling really good. I could not imagine that I could feel even better. But I did, from the comforting feeling of Love. The fear in my solar plexus disappeared and was replaced by the comfort of Love. I was grateful to the guides and Charles for providing their service.

In mid-December, Charles asked us in class how we would summarize what we had learned in the last six months. I said that I had learned how to meditate. I had learned to recognize whether I was acting from my mind, my emotions, or my spirit (Higher Self) and the effect my reactions had on my body. I was also becoming more aware of the nuances of vibrations around and in me. It was becoming comfortable and familiar to relate on that level.

Next, we did a guided meditation where I went to a meadow with the green grass. There was a gazebo there and a large chair for me. I met two guides, the same ones from the blue chair activation. I felt them merge into me. I was filled with the warm, comforting feelings of Love and Healing. I asked them what their role was in my life. They answered that this had been an introduction, and that when I felt their presence in me in the future, it would be time for me to do some kind of work. They were there to support me.

After, Charles said I needed to create a relationship with my guides, actually have a conversation with them. Get more personal with them.

Later in the evening, an entity merged with each of us, as a "gift". I felt it as having the qualities of an angel—very soft and smooth. I could feel it working on me and making adjustments in my field. I felt very light and joyous in the end.

Charles talked about three purposes of meditation:

- For repair—by developing awareness of our minds, bodies, and feelings, we can recognize, mend, and eliminate unhealthy patterns of behavior.
- For balance—by bringing the mind, body, and emotions into balance and harmony, we can benefit from their cohesion as we perform our daily tasks.
- For accessing/infusion—by dwelling in the peace and serenity of the Higher Self, we can fill ourselves with its vibration and recognize it as our natural state. Its resonance has a tremendously beneficial effect on our general wellbeing.

On December 31, this last day of the year, I felt compelled to meditate. I felt a strong activation of energy and great happiness and joy in my heart.

I sat to meditate and began in my regular, orderly way. I brought down the pillar of light. After, I felt myself being carried up the beam of light toward Source. It felt very easy. I went up, past my ball of light, past the ecstatic state of the twelfth chakra, until I arrived in a place that felt very fine and subtle, smooth and expansive. I lost the feeling of vibration here. It felt very quiet, like a buffer zone between the realm below and the one above. I sensed the qualities of timelessness and infinity in these realms, which set them apart from the temporal earth experience. I was reminded of the feelings of timelessness and infinity I experienced during my out-of-body experience at the age of 19.

I continued on beyond that level. I sensed the vibration return in my energy, and I connected with Source. I merged with Source and saw myself as pure energy and began to *spin*. This action sent a vibration outward into the cosmos and the vibration had its own signature characteristic/identity of energy. Then I recognized the same action taking place in all the planets in the cosmos! Each was spinning and they were giving out their individual vibrations, like a song, creating a melody. How beautiful and alive! This realization affected me profoundly, and I felt humbled by its synergy.

At the dawning of this New Year, I felt as though the end of my classes with Charles was nearing. I felt sad to know that I would be moving on, but also knew that many great experiences awaited me in the new cycle to come. I had grown fond of the warmth and familiarity of the group. I felt honored to have been able to learn from Charles, and so grateful for his patience, love, and dedication. I was also grateful for his shared gifts of experience and wisdom. My heart felt forever in debt to him.

Ever since I was a teenager, I have often been able to sense the ending of cycles and the nearing of new ones. Change was in the air. Although the new cycle did not manifest until the following year, I began to prepare myself with renewed diligence to my practice. In hindsight, I can see that events that were beyond my direct awareness were beginning to set in motion the chain of opportunities that would lead me to my new environment.

My focus this month was to become more aware of the *nuances* of feelings as I moved my attention through my chakras. I also practiced feeling my environment through my light body in a more sensitive and conscious way. Finally, I focused on being aware of the presence of my guides.

Continuing the theme of the mid-December class, I reflected on the year that was ending. I was now familiar with the process of being a multidimensional being. Not only was I a physical being, I was also a spiritual being with a Higher Self and light bodies that could sense with a heightened awareness and deeper wisdom. I now experienced higher vibrational states that could directly transform my physical body with their healing and balancing energies.

Through resonance, I could attune myself to other realms of existence and interact with the intelligent beings that reside there. I could also connect to the presence of others in proximity and at a distance, tuning into their physical, emotional, and mental beings, and their Higher Selves, sending them healing attunements. And finally, I was now more aware of the different characters of my chakras, as wellsprings of inner potential, just waiting to be discovered.

I remembered being taught in Catholic school about our guardian angels and how they watch over us. I had thought that it was a more of a children's story than reality, but I now sensed the presence of my guides. They were there with us all the time to serve us, help us, and guide us. Yes, we are never alone.

Chapter 6

The New Year

In January, I practiced being more aware of the present moment, the quality of the moment. How did it feel energetically? What did I sense in my surroundings? What was I feeling at exactly that moment within myself? Why was I feeling that way? Where was I feeling it: in my body, my heart, my thoughts?

What amused me was that the present was forever being renewed with a new present moment. It was alive and dynamic. There was no such thing as a good or bad day. There was only *this* present followed by another *this* present. How rich my day became!

After a class one day, I thought to myself that, as part of this new year, I needed to plan more what I wanted to get out of these classes. I needed to fill in some gaps in my learning. Charles was always there wanting to know how he could serve us. I knew that this would not last forever. I needed to benefit from these teachings while I could.

Charles had talked with us about developing relationships with our guides. They were there all the time, to serve and help us with guidance.

As my last observations for the night, I reminded myself:

I get what I need to learn from.

I get rewards for doing the right thing,

And neat surprises and *Grace*.

I noticed a soft and calm feeling come over me in meditations during this time period and in a couple of instances, I was aware of meeting two angels who lifted me to a high realm, so softly and gently, just so I could experience the feeling of it.

I also began doing healing meditations for others during this time. I connected with their physical bodies and noticed how they felt. I recognized the source of their imbalances and effected adjustments, at times using color vibrations, other times clearing chakras to better receive light, and sometimes applying Geometric Harmonic Configurations.

Geometric Harmonic Configurations are patterns of life. They are geometric structures that resonate a vibratory influence on the condition at hand, to enhance or reduce the present state of activity taking place within the body, promoting balance and wellbeing. They have a pattern, a form, and emanate a frequency that spans the third, fourth and fifth Dimensions (more will be covered about Dimensions in a later chapter). All of the Configurations were applied on many levels, as needed. I recognized and instinctively knew what to do.

By the end of January, I felt a new quality in the energy flow. As though there was new momentum in the flow and new dispensations of insight in the air. Charles called it a time of *acceleration* in the evolution of consciousness. This was the beginning of an active period. To facilitate the flow of energy, I needed to let go of personal agendas and allow the flow to manifest. Then I would be able to tune in to the cosmic Intelligence and receive what it had to offer during this period.

By now, it was April, and I was learning more how to work with vibrations and energy through my meditations. It seemed as though I was being presented with new insights, was seeing and understanding new concepts and ways of applying them.

For example, I had done a meditation called "Angels on Assignment." During a period of active fires occurring throughout Florida, I watched them from above and began to apply Geometric Harmonic Configurations to reestablish balance and harmony over the area. The next day, the weather changed and it rained there in the Central/Eastern part of Florida. During the exercise, I just knew the appropriate pattern to use, although I had never done it before, or even thought in that way before. I'm not saying that I made it rain, but I know that the exercise helped balance the region, in the same way as it did when I was doing healings during meditation.

I had another insightful meditation, where I learned the true purpose of focused meditation; to train the mind to hold the energetic space. During this meditation, I was led by a guide to be in the presence of another being or group of beings. I could feel their presence in the realm, although I could not see them physically. They began to project a *feeling*, a *tone* that I had never felt before. It was solemn, with a depth of wisdom, but without specific embodiment—only a pure abstract concept of it. I became aware that I was sustaining the tone to set the atmosphere, *for someone else* to stop, pause, and reflect. That was my job at that moment. This was a new experience for me.

Chapter 7
The Jesus Meditation

Near the end of April, Charles led us in a guided meditation. The premise was that we were going to see Jesus during his life. Since there is a recorded history of Jesus, we were asked to go back in time and view him during the period of his life on Earth. I had never thought of going back in time to see Jesus, of all people! I could not even fathom what the event would be like in reality.

Later in the evening when I returned home, I went straight to my notebook and wrote my impressions of the meditation.

> *I went back, back, back in time to a place where Jesus was present. I saw him among a crowd of people. I went inside the body of an old woman, about seventy years old, short, stocky and old looking, and she was looking at Jesus. I saw Jesus through her experience. He was next to her in a crowd, walking by her. She saw his face and was struck by* **the look in his eyes***. They say that the eyes are the window to the soul. When you looked at his eyes, you could see so much goodness . . . . It was a look with depth that went beyond, a look that made you realize that you were in the presence of greatness, a depth in him that made you feel that if he looked at you, you would* **know** *that all is possible, that all Truths would be known, that all questions would be answered, that*

all realizations would be understood, that the greatest of Love would be felt, that the deepest compassion would be expressed. A look like no one present had ever seen in another man, but most of all, a goodness that transcends all.

*When in that presence, all **know** that they have seen Jesus!*

Viewing Jesus through the old woman, I felt like a witness to the event, living it through her experience.

Chapter 8

The Haunted House

In early May of 1999, I went to a haunted house with a group from the Florida Parapsychological Research Association. I was curious to see if I could pick up impressions there.

I met Dave, one of the members, at City College and we drove out in the country on this warm, sunny day. After about a half-hour drive, we arrived at an old house at the end of a private country road. It appeared to have been built in the early 1800s. It was surrounded by old oak trees that grow all over this area of North Florida.

There were already other cars from our group parked in the driveway by the side of the house. As soon as I opened the car door and set my feet on the ground, I noticed that my legs and feet felt as though they were tingling and I had the eerie feeling that I was floating toward the house, instead of just walking— as though my feet were so light that I they didn't touch the ground. I walked into the house and immediately felt altered, the kind of feeling that I would get during meditation night at Charles's. I wondered for a moment if I was just imagining these feelings, but no, I was definitely altered.

I looked to my left and saw a living room/dining room. The team leader was beginning to prepare the room for our séance, and Dave joined him with some electronic equipment he had brought along. Group members were milling about, speaking among themselves on the ground floor, and several psychics who would attempt to communicate with the spirit present in the house were there. I could see auras and feel the density of the air in the meeting room. I could make out etheric patterns by the corner of the room where a sofa bed was.

I went to the bathroom to refresh myself from the drive. When I returned to the main room, I had missed the introductory story given by the home's owner so I didn't know any background history about the house. As we waited to go upstairs for a tour of the home, I looked around the area to get my bearings. The bathroom was located in a room behind the vestibule, and a white door led to the back of the house and the kitchen. The rooms to the right were living quarters. The large living/dining area on the left was square and had a dining room table in the middle. There was a piano on the right, a lounge sofa in the left corner and, facing a window between them, a small table with artifacts on it.

But what really struck me was the clash between the stately old house and the décor. The residents of the house, a bearded man and his girlfriend, who raised potbelly pigs in the back yard, had turned the vestibule hall area into a bar atmosphere with stools, NASCAR miniature cars on the right wall shelf, a dart board, and bottles on the shelf behind a bar. A set of speakers was playing rock and roll, while the white plastic bust of a mannequin wearing lingerie, one breast showing, looked on. An old antique-looking phone sat on a small table with a sign that said, "Phone – leave 25 cents."

We went up a flight of stairs and visited the rooms on the second level to pick up psychic impressions. I felt that there was an unusual quality about the two rooms upstairs, located directly above the main room downstairs. But I was not able to describe my impressions at the time because I had nothing to compare the feeling to. This was new to me.

As we followed the owner back down the stairs, he continued his story about the history of the house, mentioning that a family had lived there around the period of the Civil War. One day, the wife was walking down the steps, and she fell to the bottom, hit her head on the floor, and lost consciousness. She was then carried over to the lounge bed in the adjoining room, where she died. Local folks believed that she might have been pushed down the stairs during an argument with her husband. The house had been haunted by the woman ever since.

We returned to join the leader of our group, who was finishing setting up scientific instruments in the main room. We sat at the table and began the séance by touching hands to build up our collective energy. Then people started to describe their impressions. The person next to me began to speak to the woman haunting the house. He spoke with her for a few minutes, and then he mentioned that she was moving toward the piano. The moment he said that, I felt a deep, cold chill go through my arms. The kind that goes right to the bone. I was freezing! For the next thirty minutes, I felt it intermittently throughout my arms, hands, and legs.

I focused on the woman and saw her spirit. I asked for help from my guides, and two came to assist me. I approached her in my light body along with the two guides. I tried to open her chakras, calm her energy, and connect her with Source. She was agitated by the presence of the group. Several people were speaking with her now, questioning her about her reasons for remaining in the house.

She was surprised to be conversing with someone. She was not used to any interactions, even less with someone talking to her! I realized that when we had first arrived at the house, she had come outside and was feeling upset and apprehensive about the presence of strangers on her property. All these people arriving at her house!

After some work, my guides and I succeeded in filling her with the white light from Source. She looked up and recognized Source, but only for an instant. She snapped her attention back as if saying, "NO!" Her mind jumped back into a pattern of rationalizations that she played over and over again.

The leader of the group began speaking to her, and she felt scolded like a little girl. She began to cry. She was hiding a secret, a reason to feel deep sadness in her heart and hold on to this memory that kept her here. I told the team leader that with her thought patterns in place, she was not going anywhere. She would not leave this house.

I heard her explain to us that she had remained at the house after her death because she was worried about her daughter and young son. When she spoke, I realized that I was listening to a country woman from the 1800s. She had little education and thought with the mentality of the times.

Her husband, she said, had been a successful merchant during the Civil War. That was how they were able to live in this grand house. However, he was often angry and had a violent temper. As the local legend said, he had hit her when she was coming down the stairs. Then she lost her footing and fell down the stairs, hitting her head on the floor. She died shortly after. She explained again that she had stayed in the house because she was worried about her two children who remained. As I listened to her, I thought to myself that she did not realize that her children were all dead now and that over one hundred years had passed. She was no longer in the 1800s. These were modern times.

I felt her heart and began to cry. I knew that I could not change her outlook. It was her free will to be the way she was. She was going to stay as long as she wanted. At least, she saw a glimpse of Source.

During our drive back home, I asked Dave to turn on the heater in the car. I was still freezing. He turned to me and said, "You got the *chills*!"

I asked him of his impressions. He said that he had also felt altered the entire time he was there and had been almost unable to speak. He said he had struggled to set up the scientific equipment, had been quiet, and felt as in a daze. Then we talked about whether the woman's Higher Self could help to bring her to Source and he said, of course, the Higher Self was there, "but do we listen to our Higher Selves?" Who knows how to reason with someone?

I also told him that I had felt nauseated in my stomach when I was there. He said that was why everyone was drinking so much soda, to settle their stomachs and to get grounded.

I've learned over the years that the feeling of nausea is caused by the rapid change of energetic density taking place in my body. For example, if I return too quickly at the end of a guided meditation or soul travel, or after experiencing another being, I might experience slight nausea. It can be compared to the way a passenger in an airplane might feel after an abrupt change in altitude.

Chapter 9

Looking for a Compassionate Person

For the last three years, I had worked in an art studio as a production artist. I enjoyed the company of an eclectic group of people and looked forward to working there every day. Our company's owner would travel throughout the country, attending trade shows and returning with new orders for us to fill. Somehow, it kept us busy enough until the next orders. However, competition in the industry was tough and we all knew that our jobs were dependent on sales generated through arts and crafts shows. Now we were beginning to hear that "made in America" was being threatened by the influx of low-cost Chinese products that were encroaching on our market. It was only a matter of time until we would no longer be able to compete with them in the marketplace.

By the end of spring, the owner gathered us all together and announced to us that after sixteen years in business, he could no longer remain competitive unless he moved his entire operation to China. American production costs could no longer keep up with the lower prices. He made arrangements so that we could apply for retraining benefits if we chose to do so. Several people opted for clerical or other courses. Although we all qualified for unemployment benefits, I chose to look for another job.

By May, I was interviewing with several companies. Pay was low in this area. Living in a college town kept the wages low because employers could always hire students at entry-level rates. Although I had over a decade of experience in the hospitality industry, I could not find employment for more than slightly above minimum wage.

One day I saw an ad that said, "Looking for compassionate person."

"Well," I thought, "That's me!"

So I made an appointment for an interview. I walked in, with my most professional dressed-for-success attire. I was led to a conservative office and sat in a leather chair. Across the desk in front of me sat a woman with a warm smile, who reached out her hand and said, "Hi! I'm Donna."

She began explaining the job to me. I must say that I had no idea what I had just walked into. She was the head of Family Services for a funeral home and cemetery. As I listened and listened to her explaining the particulars of the job, with that winning smile, I thought, "No way!" She was obviously enthusiastic about it, but I wasn't. Then she asked if I had any questions. What kind of questions did she think I might have? Maybe I wanted to make arrangements for myself? You must be kidding. How could I talk to anyone about that? I said, "I don't know . . . ."

So she said, "Think about it . . . If you think of anything or want to ask me anything, just give me a call."

I left, just glad to get out of there.

I went home and kept looking for work. And I started thinking of that nice woman. "Someone has to do that job," I thought. I'm really good with people. In some ways, it's not that different from the hospitality business. I had handled group sales. I was used to people coming in from out of town for a wedding or graduation, needing organization and direction. It was usually a hectic time for everyone. I enjoyed being able to make their visit smoother. In a way, this was not so different.

I called her back. She made some time for me, and I went back and asked her a few questions. She gave me more details about the job. The job took place at the cemetery. I would meet with the family when there had been a death and go over any arrangements that might have been made previously or finish up the final details. I would go over burial site details, set the date and time for the funeral ceremony, and talk about the final wishes. On the day of the funeral I would meet them at the church, stay for the service, and follow them to the graveside afterward. I would witness the burial and sign the final documents for the State. A month later, I would follow up with the spouse or family member and provide them with referrals to grief counseling services in the area.

I left the office, still thinking, "No way! It's just too weird. I'm not going to do *that*!"

Well, to this day, I don't know what made me take that job. Maybe it was because I *am* a compassionate person. I knew I could do the job and that it would feel rewarding to do it. Maybe it was Donna's nice, warm smile . . . What I did not know was that it would contribute much to my spiritual development during the months and year that followed.

I started my new job at the beginning of June.

Chapter 10

Going Deeper

Over the next several months I continued to be diligent in my meditation practice and attend the weekly classes. When I got to *The Wall* in meditation, I found I had to dig deeper to get beyond it. I had to have the courage to be vulnerable, naked and bare to myself. It was a necessary step for me to take now. I had to be open and honest with myself, let go of my created image of myself, to find my True Self. Only then could I *feel* what was really inside me. Only then could I receive intuition/insight and feel what was really going on. Only then could I allow the Divine to work through me.

In class, we talked about the importance of knowing ourselves, which some call self-realization. I had once thought that I was a wife, a daughter, a career-woman, an artist, but when I began to meditate, I realized that I was much more than the roles I was living. Going deeper, I realized that I held a pure essence in my spirit. I could finally recognize the purer nature of my being. This self-awareness was the same one that I had felt as a child of two, and as I felt today. It was so close to me, yet I had not seen it. My pure essence resonated its own note, flavor and beauty. I also recognized that every living thing has its own, unique and pure expression within it. The more I connected with Source during meditation, the more strongly I felt my True Self. There was a link between this loving presence that permeated all of creation and my self-awareness. I felt myself as a manifestation of Source. It was humbling because I also saw others the same way. When we know our Selves, we no longer harbor anger in our hearts because we are able to also see the beauty in others. When we are connected to Source we have an unlimited reserve of love to give to others, and when we are connected to Source, we feel supported in any situation. I realized how we are each responsible for how we choose to express our True Self; our gifts, talents abilities; our intention, wishes; our love and compassion.

I saw that there are many layers of the Self. They can be compared to a Russian doll; the outer doll holds within it another, and another, and another inner doll. In a similar way, there is the Self that is choosing to be active on Earth, the Higher Self that is connected to a greater purpose, the even Higher Selves that exist actively in other realms, and an even larger encompassing Self that is no longer individual, but integrated into the wholeness of God/Source. I felt deep gratitude for the Grace that enabled these realizations.

Charles was aware of the progress of my meditations and my sensitivity to higher dimensions. In early July he had me channel in class. I channeled a male being. I felt my body density change and become heavier. The spirit felt solid and grounded like a rock. I was struck by the contrast between his presence and mine. He felt very solemn and intensely focused. His presence was palpable and I could *feel* that he was a very developed being, that he was very spiritually conscious and strong in character. His physical density was immovable/solid, and he was emotionally secure and intellectually superior to me. In contrast, when I giggled at some point during the exercise, I was very aware of my lightness and immature level of spiritual development. I felt humble in his presence. This was no joking matter.

The back of my head felt as though energy was bursting from the inside out. I felt an imprint of him on all levels: spiritually, mentally, physically, and emotionally. Charles said we are forever changed by the experience. He called it a *dispensation*. It is as a gift of insight, to merge so fully with another. I felt his soul, his Wisdom, with total purity and transparency. By experiencing the depth and breadth of his soul, I perceive it as a revelation. Now, each time I channel or meet another spirit being, I experience it in the same way. Those meetings occur on a telepathic level where nothing is hidden. I once mentioned to a friend how wonderful it would be if we all communicated in this way on Earth.

Someone asked Charles if this was what he experienced all the time . . . He smiled and said, "Welcome to my world." I was so grateful that Charles had made this possible for us tonight. He was so attentive and loving of us all. I always was and continue to be awed by his genuine dedication as a teacher as he helped facilitate the process.

Later in the evening I asked to channel messages of healing and upliftment for those who may need it in my work at the cemetery.

On one occasion, Charles showed us a list of qualities and asked us to choose one to meditate on. I was attracted to the word *order*. We did a breathing exercise for a few minutes to clear our heads, and then I began to contemplate the word *order*.

I realized that when I had done spiritual/physical healings, I was putting a person's molecular pattern back into order. That was what I needed to do to *me*!

Charles said to reflect on all of the facets and qualities, of our chosen word. He said to notice it in everything we saw, everything we did, notice it in the people we met, everywhere. Really think about it.

It was what I needed to understand right now.

The following week, Charles channeled Llokma, a middle-eastern spiritual teacher. I mentioned to the teacher that I felt good but also insecure about my new job at the cemetery. I wondered if he could explain my mixed feelings. He had me analyze myself by asking:

- Is my Higher Self OK with my new job? I answered yes.
- Is my body OK with it (the way my chakras react)? I answered yes.
- Is it my Inner Child that is insecure? I answered yes.

He advised, "The best way to treat a child who is insecure is to give it Satsang. Ask for answers from your Higher Self. In meditation, ask for words of wisdom, or ask to be guided to a special book or person that can provide the answer you seek. It will bring your Inner Child peace."

Since then, I've often remembered to look for comfort in Satsang.

On another occasion during class, I asked Charles how to feel the presences more physically when channeling. I noticed that during meditation, I had a tendency to float upward due to my light nature. He sat me in the blue chair. It was only my second time, and I immediately felt altered.

He brought down two entities. As I channeled the first one, my lips had trouble speaking, I felt distant, and my voice sounded distant. I was not used to vocalizing and had stepped out of my body to observe. It was difficult to experience the entity and speak simultaneously. The second entity, John, was one I had tried to connect with the previous night in meditation. Instead of the distance I felt with the first entity, I was aware of how John's physical presence changed the way my body's vitality felt. I felt his *weight* inside my molecules. I felt full, like a cloud. I really liked him.

Charles asked me a few questions and the answers came visually and with words. Charles asked about the truck he wanted to purchase at that time. I saw it in my mind: it was a light grey/blue pickup truck, 1980s model. The process of answering was funny to me. I would receive the answer *through* John and then try to answer *for* him, although he was providing the answers (letting go does not come naturally). When I had watched Charles channel, he got completely out of the way, as he had done with Llokma the previous week, and the visiting being conversed directly. I noticed that I tended to simply converse with higher teachers in the higher realms during meditation in the same way as I would sit with a friend and have a talk. That was, and still is, my personal preference.

Charles gave me some instruction on things I needed to remember when channeling:

Focus on holding the energy of the being that is inside me, to assist him.

- Let go of Paula, so that I'm not too busy analyzing and questioning what is going on.
- Concentrate on harmonizing my chakras and allowing the combined energy to rise through the opening at the top of my head.
- Feel the entity come down in the same way. Feel the tingle in the back of my head and neck.
- Close up the entrance when I finish.
- Always be systematic and orderly throughout the procedure. Open in the spirit of Love, close and end the experience.

He also reassured me that I could still hear and control my body. I would be lending my body from *my* free will. The beings would assist me in my personal growth, I would assist them in their missions. It was a two-way gift. "You will feel a little different. Like you got an 'adjustment,' like going to the chiropractor. Like a major Shakti-pat!"

Charles ended the session in orderly manner.

At the end of July, Charles had us meditate to a piece of music by Bach called "*Air,*" very light and beautiful.

I first saw myself go up through the top of my head and then I thought of doing it again from there, splitting upward through the top of my head, then moving up and doing it again and again, with all the me's sitting on top of each other, as I had done before.

Next I made a blue/purple bubble and wrapped it around all of the Me's. I looked up and saw a bright yellow ball of light and from it a yellow beam of light came down through all of the Me's, down to the Earth. Then I thought of wrapping my energy all around the whole room, enveloping all the people in the group.

After the meditation, Charles said that I caused everyone to follow me up on top of the building! I was surprised to hear him say that. I did not know that acting that way would affect people. Many people said that they were aware of an angel above them and they followed it. I didn't think of myself that way. It is interesting how we interpret the sight of etheric beings. In the subtle realms, we all appear in our purified form. I realized that I needed to be aware of the way I *affect* and *effect* people now that I was connected to the Light of Source.

Once again, I saw that it was not what service I did that was important but more *who* I was and *how* I expressed my presence. I remembered that we each have our own unique quality and that our true purpose is to share it with others.

To be connected to Source and be happy, I told myself, that was the essential. From there, the rest would fall in place.

Illustration: I Wrapped My Energy Around the Room

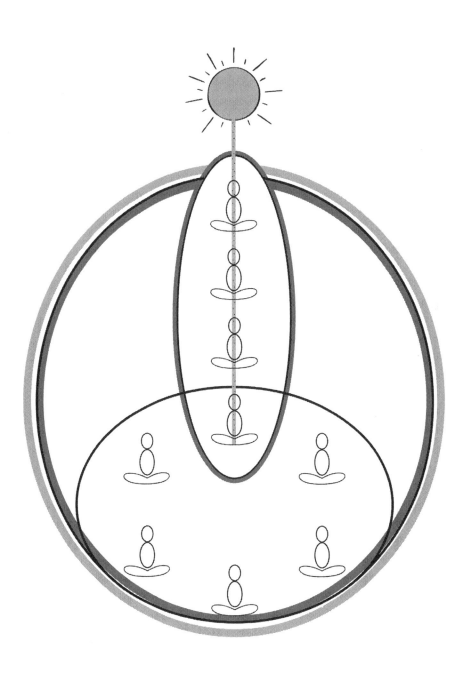

I Wrapped My Energy Around the Room

Chapter 11

Energetic Vibration

I continued to make peace with my past, healing my heart and letting go of sadness and grief. I made a resolution to be optimistic.

Charles said, "Ask for a good day. When you go to bed at night, ask to have joy in your heart when you awake. Look forward to the day with its surprises and miracles. Plan something fun for yourself when you first awake. Ask your guides if you need an idea."

I noticed the quality of my vibrational tone and learned how it interacted within the higher realms' resonances. Each realm has its own vibration, its reason for being and purpose, be it only to satisfy a creative expression. It is like each unique musical note and each shade of color in the spectrum expressing a nuance of the whole. My body had its own signature, energetic vibration. It was harmonious with other beings with similar vibration and was mutually attracted in a sympathetic way.

We already function on many levels simultaneously, whether we are aware of it or not. We are all multidimensional beings.

One day, I was extinguishing a vanilla candle and burned my finger. I took a white stone, selenite, and pointed it to my finger sending light blue light and Love. Suddenly, the stinging was gone! My finger became full of healing energy. I then finished the healing with white light and Love. I had done it! I somehow had always known that I could use the white stone in healing.

Stones have the property to amplify our own resonance.

Charles said that some spirits are so high that you cannot channel them through your body. They can only be reached in the higher realms. You have to go there to connect with them. I confirmed this fact in later meditations. I was taken on occasion to some of those realms by a guide.

I asked Charles, "How do you know if your guides are there for you all the time?"

So he asked me, "Who do you love?" (My former husband)

"Does your love span all time?" (Yes)

"It is the same for your guides. They are not limited by time. They always love you and are always there to listen to you and to help you. There is no *time*. You are the one who is preoccupied with your life down here and does not have time for them. But they are always there to listen when you take time to acknowledge them."

In late August, I tuned in to the part of me that is *beyond* my Higher Self, the one who is always lucid in the higher realms, the part of me that is super clear in my highest meditations. I had experienced that sense of higher perspective on many occasions, along with its expansive sense of calmness and timelessness. Now I realized that, having experienced that higher state, I could connect and act from that heightened awareness. I also realized that a part of me holds a presence there and has been there all along. I opened my eyes like we do in class and tried to function in the real world from there. "Need to practice," I thought to myself. "That's the place to be."

I realized that the wider the range of awareness, the deeper the understanding. That was how to live with multidimensional presence.

In early September I visited a second haunted house with members of the Florida Parapsychological Research Association. This house was known to have friendly ghosts and had been studied extensively. The current occupants were a couple in their early forties and their school-age children.

This was a continuing research project planned by the association and conducted through the local community college. I was participating in this study along with other students. We were asked to enter each room one at a time and write on a sheet of paper our impressions of the room. We were to note whether we sensed a presence in the room or noticed temperature differences, then choose from a list of qualities those that best described the presence and indicate where in the room the impressions were noticed. I sensed two active ghosts in the house and residual impressions from past members of the family.

In the parlor and old sewing room upstairs I sensed a woman, who would have been the mother. She was nice, loving, warm, and gentle. I saw residual impressions of young children running and playing upstairs between their adjoining bedrooms. There was much laughter as the mother tended to her work in the sewing room.

On the main floor, there was a small office with a fireplace called the Civil War room. I immediately noticed the presence of a man in that room—stern, serious, strict, severe, negative in attitude. I first sensed him standing in front of the fireplace and indicated it on my sheet of paper. Then I noticed him by the window, and then in front of the desk. I finally realized that he was following me around the room! I smiled and made a note of it. I also noticed that the room felt much colder than other rooms in the house.

I was pleased that I was able to pick up impressions, as it was difficult to concentrate because on this day, A & E (Arts and

Entertainment Channel) was there filming a documentary on haunted houses and ghosts. They had their crew, bright lights, and cameras set up throughout the residence. Although they were being quiet, I had to focus not to be distracted.

After our group had finished going through the house and our notes had been collected for later analysis, the current owner of the house briefed us on its history. Yes indeed, a family had lived there with young children. Upstairs there had been two bedrooms, one for the parents and one for the children, and adjoining it was a sewing room used by the mother. The study downstairs was the father's office. The owner also mentioned that the office was fifteen degrees cooler than any other room in the house and there was no explanation for it.

I found this visit interesting and was pleased with the validation I gained from the owner's history and personal account of the home. I was also pleased that I was able to test my ability to tune in to the vibrations present and could differentiate between the active presence of spirits and residual impressions from past events.

In September I continued attending meditation classes. During the guided meditation one evening we listened again to Bach's "*Air*." I could feel Charles's spiritual presence in the room as he visited each of us. I knew when it was my turn, when he gave me an energetic attunement, and then moved on the person next to me. I followed him and was aware of where his spirit body was in the room. I mentioned it during our group debriefing after the meditation and he acknowledged my observation. Others had also been aware of his presence during the meditation.

Later in the week, I did a self-guided meditation and met my spirit guide in a garden. We sat in a gazebo and I asked him about work. He said that the reason I was doing sales was to help open up my throat chakra. It did not matter where I worked as long as I did some sales for the next few months, to learn to talk and communicate verbally. He also said that I needed to exercise to strengthen my spine and back muscles. The all-round fitness would benefit me in the long run. That was all I needed to focus and work on right now. I always received the answers from a big picture view.

In October I began a course of study to become a minister through the Alliance of Divine Love in Florida. This organization was very active in the community and still is today. Its membership is made up of professional practitioners in various disciplines, including therapists, health care workers, lawyers, social workers, and counselors. All students taking the program have a deep sense of humanity and spiritual commitment.

The ministerial program was an accelerated course that usually lasted two years, in addition to a year of community service. I had wondered if I really had the time to undertake the training, since I had a deep feeling that change was coming and that I might be leaving the area next spring. But somehow I sensed that I would have time to complete the program. It helped that I did not need to perform community service, since I was already working full-time at the funeral home/cemetery providing emotional support and service for families during their time of sorrow.

Near the end of the month Charles channeled Phillip. He specialized in questions about spiritual development. I told him that I had been through many changes in the last few years, spiritually and in my environment, and now felt as though I was sitting still. I asked him what was going on.

He answered that I had been put "on hold," like taking a bookmark, turning it upside down, and putting it back in the book. Some plans were being made for me and in the meantime, I was being kept spiritually occupied so as not to lose my spiritual connection. I knew all that I needed to know right then. I was awake and aware, and would be called upon when the time was right. In time, I would understand why. "Just sit still for now and enjoy. All is good and the guides are watching over you.

Yes indeed, I did not know what was awaiting me just a few months later, in spring of 2000. I would be called upon to serve and very quickly, a new chapter would begin for me. But now, it was time for me to wait while events were being prepared for the change. The ministerial program was just the perfect course of study for me at this time.

As I got close to the end of my first notebook, I felt that I was on the verge of a breakthrough. Something was about to happen, something bright and promising.

In class one night, Charles channeled a being whose job was to radiate his energy out into the universe. I knew what the being meant when he described it. I had done something similar during meditation. He radiated his essence to make spiritual adjustments, in a similar way that a chiropractor makes a correction in the physical body. This was only the being's seventh or eighth time experiencing a physical body. He mentioned that my understanding of duality would change as I went through a rapid growth in the next three or four months.

I paused to review my life in the last couple of days of September, to examine my progression and development and see how I had planned all the little steps I had taken toward personal development. I had always been shy and insecure and had worked to overcome those feelings all my life, a little at a time. I looked back at how far I had come and what I had accomplished.

I was beginning to finally believe that I could do anything that I set myself to do. Really believe it. With work, I could do it, one step at a time. I was also learning the value of letting go. Although I was comfortable with going with the flow, I was also consciously aware that there was a higher plan being prepared for me. As Charles kept reminding us, "Not my will, but God's will."

In a prayer I thanked my guides, my friends and kindred spirits, for helping me along the way. I thanked them all for caring. I vowed to work every day to not disappoint them. If I should transgress, it was only so that I may learn to grow. I thanked them all for their blessings and wished them Love and eternal peace.

May Divine Love be with you always.

III

The Teachings

Chapter 1

Overlapping Dimensions

In October I did a self-guided meditation:

I picked up my wand (a combination of crystals and stones attached to a copper tube with gold-plated wire) and went up and far for a long time, travelling far, far away.

I stopped and began to feel where I was. I knew that it no longer would be a linear experience. I began to roll forward as though *folding into* something, as though walking into a seashell. I began to be aware of the energetic quality of planes of energy. I saw a veil/cloud of blue molecules passing through a cloud of another different color. This was a *representation* of two dimensions existing simultaneously, yet separately. I was also aware that a third and a fourth dimension could also exist simultaneously the same way. I sensed that I could access a finer dimension by first progressing through an intermediary first. Of course, any dimension can be accessed directly by tuning to its frequency.

I tried to see how a blended dimension would feel, how its quality and experience would have its own signature (identifiable flavor/feel) and how it's time, if any, would be altered.

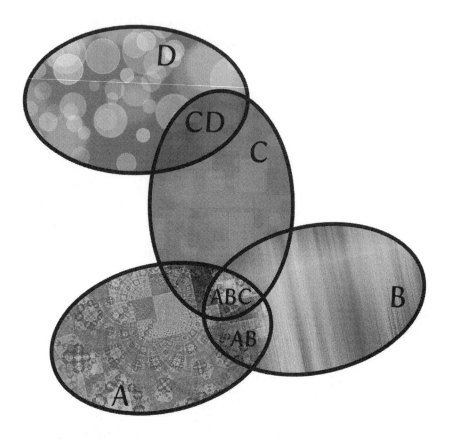

Overlapping Dimensions

1) Two dimension interlocking (AB).
2) Three dimensions simultaneously
   intermingling (ABC).
3) Other dimension D can be reached by crossing C.

Chapter 2

The Dimensions & the Chakras

I noticed a relationship between the chakras and dimensions of awareness. Although each of us is unique and will experience the dimensions and chakras according to our own nature, I was beginning to find that, for me, the dimensions and chakras interacted and coexisted in the following general way.

We are familiar with the first three dimensions through geometry: the point leading to the line, creating form and mass in the third dimension, with its innate resonance, frequency, amplitude, and influence on its environment.

The expression of the Fourth Dimension introduces intuition, awareness, and consciousness. It is associated with the primary chakras and access to the eighth and ninth chakras. Our bodies in the Third and Fourth Dimensions are made up particles that are dependent on the Earth realm.

The expression of the Fifth Dimension is correspondence—the dynamic interaction, relationship, between two states of matter. Here, our bodies begins to lose density and are transformed into pure energy. We are able to interact with other forms of energy. We can attract energy through resonance, perform healings and communicate with higher beings. This

Dimension is associated with the tenth and eleventh chakras where unlimited worlds exist.

The expression of the Sixth Dimension is the state of no-mind, only presence. It is the nature of presence, timeless and ever present. This is the core foundation and found in all the chakras. It can be experienced in its pure form in the twelfth chakra.

These descriptions are only general and may be modified in endless ways as they interact with each other (as in *Overlapping Dimensions*).

I had become aware of my Fifth Dimensional development, recalling the past year's experiences:

- Healing with colors
- Using Geometric Harmonic Configurations
- Accessing higher realms

I remember many times during meditation when I could not go further and had to change the language, the communication/perception pattern, I used to better tune in to a new frequency. I told Charles tonight, "It's like going from simple mathematics to calculus. It was as though I were doing spiritual calculus during the guided meditation tonight."

I was just learning. I had a lot to learn still. Charles said to contact a teaching guide who could communicate with me, and me with him/or her. The guide would "bring me along" on my development. I realized that night that I had grown a lot over the previous eighteen months, since I had begun to meditate. Thank you all for your benevolence. I was grateful to all my teachers.

Chapter 3

Meditation and Grace

I had learned to feel crystals in the last year and notice their individual characteristics. I was using them now during meditation to become attuned to the finer frequencies. I had been thinking lately how crystals are like spiritual cocktails. When I develop enough sensitivity to feel their always-so-subtle (sometimes really powerful!) nuances, they can enhance or facilitate a mind-state. I was gaining more refinement and ability to sense them. It is similar to developing a taste for various wines: it is something that evolves over time with experience.

Also in October I conducted my first group guided meditation for Group Spirit, a social organization created for the purpose of discussing spiritual topics and meeting others with common interests. Several people I knew were there. Among them, Ted made a breakthrough in his meditation. He was able to separate his Higher Self from his mind. He was clear and quiet. He said that he could do it again on his own now. Joanne went to the ball of light and felt so good that she didn't want to come back.

I thought to myself; "I thank you guides for your supervision. I realized that it is only with their Grace that we advance to the higher realms. Thank you. I am very grateful."

I've often had spontaneous realizations over the years and I am always grateful for them. In those times, I receive them as gifts, gifts of Grace.

Breakthroughs, realizations, and awakenings are all gifts of Grace.[2]

Who or what do you thank for them?

In class we talked about energy patterns—the ones that, if not connected to Source, become polarized and stagnant, such as: feeling depressed, in a rut, angry, or frustrated. We were encouraged to locate those feelings in our bodies. Which chakras were they associated with? Then we connected to our light energy, from the ball of light, and used it to clear those blocks. Sometimes deep insights arose and blocks could be released.

Charles spoke about our *kundalini*, a Sanskrit word for the body's life force. The chakras are connected to the *shushumna*, or central, channel, along the spinal cord, where the *kundalini* rises from the root chakra in the form of a double helix that stimulates each chakra as it rises, allowing the whole to become exalted. This inner life force is already in our body, waiting to be awakened. (In medicine, the caduceus used to symbolize healing, depicts the active *kundalini* serpents.)

---

2   A video discussing The State of Grace is available at
    www.paulaforget.com/inspired. It is an excerpt from Masters of the
    Journey Video Conference featuring Paula Forget, November 18, 2015.

Chapter 4
Dorothy & the Meditator-for-Hire

In early November, Charles had me channel. There were two other people there who attended the class.

The first being I channeled was called Dorothy. She was very light and cheerful. Her job was to watch over children. She protected and encouraged the lightness in children. "They should never be burdened and weighed down, but encouraged to enjoy the lightness that is their being." Dorothy also worked with mothers and women who watch over children by inspiring them in their selection of activities.

The air around her felt sunny and light. I asked her if she had any advice for anyone in the room and she recommended to one in the group concentrate on his third eye area and it would lighten his heart.

Then I channeled "the Meditator-For-Hire," as I liked to refer to him. I knew it was him when he arrived. He was very serious and humorless (although Charles did make him laugh hard a couple of times). He felt heavy and weighed down and his bottom lip curled out. He talked about his job. He was to maintain a tone, to establish stability. He was also a healer. It occurred to me that he had been teaching me healing techniques all along.

Charles then asked him a question that he did not know the answer to. So Charles asked him to ask others who could provide an answer. Then suddenly, my perception completely changed. As I was experiencing the Meditator-For-Hire's thoughts, I felt myself rising to another realm where I saw and felt swirls of light that were white and blue. I was curious about the realm he went to, but had never experienced his consciousness in such a higher state. I realized that I was seeing a truer aspect of his spiritual essence. It felt really good and made me smile. As I was enjoying the realm, I suddenly realized that I had completely forgotten about him. He had returned to our class and was completing his conversation with Charles. I left the white and blue realm and apologetically reconnected with the Meditator-For-Hire. Then the session was over and he left.

I was thankful to Charles for suggesting that I try to channel. I really enjoyed it. The beings are so interesting to experience.

Chapter 5

Bruce

Throughout November I channeled several entities.

During a self-guided meditation, I channeled Bruce. He was a male human spirit, with a very physical presence. I was very aware of his body type, which felt confident, fearless, and direct. He also displayed a male personality and physical character. He felt alive and easily aroused sexually. I could feel his testosterone running through my body, arms, and hands. He was very energized.

His purpose was to help me be strong and follow through on my thoughts. He found holes/gaps in the continuity of my light body due to my lack of self-confidence. He filled them in so that my physical self would have more continuity.

I thanked him for allowing me to experience him.

Afterwards, my throat and chest felt slightly nauseous from the quick change back to my body's' frequency.

Chapter 6

Four Beings, Mersia

Later in the week, I channeled one morning and noted later that I had been meditating for an hour and fifteen minutes.

So far, I had been recording my impressions after the meditations. I noticed that sometimes I was so altered that it was difficult to keep up and try to remember all that was going on. This time I tried to write the meditation as it was unfolding. That way I would not have to remember the experience and could read it later. I sat with my eyes closed and tried to visualize the clipboard with paper that was sitting on my lap. I sat comfortably and began to meditate. I channeled four beings. Here are excerpts.

I meet a Guide. She is "Transitional Helper" as she calls herself. "You need a comfortable chair to channel in. Maintain good posture". Then she said "There are too many distractions. People can't focus on what is important." (I feel a high degree of energy, as though I am moving, being propelled very fast.) "Be vigilant. Keep YOUR course. Although these are challenging times, remember the essence of what's important".

I encounter another Guide. "I was an administrator, a Civic Analyst, 1000 years ago in the Middle East, concerned with order in city government. Call me "Sam". You cannot say my name. (He is sitting, leaning to the left, head tilted to the left. I feel his density all in the left side of my body. He is a wise being with connections to the Earth plane.)

I encounter another Guide, another female. She is a motherly type. She said "Use your scrap paper to transcribe on." She means the box of old forms that I have kept, for writing on the back of.

I encounter another Guide. "Love to all, this is a joyous time that you are concerned with matters of the spirit. This is a great day for Humanity that it is consciously being given knowledge although it is through the subtle realms. It is true that there appears to be quickness in the flow of energy. It is due to the high degree of knowledge that is being dispensed at this time in many forms. I am glad that you are enjoying my visit. I can come as often as you like. My name is Mersia. I say to her, "I feel your light in the center of my heart, like a mandala, grounded and radiant, in the form of a flower mandala of love." "The feeling in your heart chakra," she says, "you will remember this."

Mersia was light and joyous, with a very loving heart. She was a higher realm being. I thanked them for their visit.

I continue to be amazed by how I perceived, and still perceive, the beings on many levels. I simultaneously *see* them, *feel* them, *know* them and *understand* them conceptually and abstractly, and *hear*, all at one time! I hoped that eventually I would be able to communicate the nuances and flavors of what I was experiencing.

I continued recording my meditations in this way from this day on. I found the text a great teaching tool to study later.

The same week, during meditation class, I returned to the ninth and tenth chakras above the top of my head.

I had noted that the ninth chakra is where Sam, the civic analyst, was from. He was providing service to the Earth plane in dealing with aspects of duality. The tenth chakra was where Mersia was from, where angels dwell in Absolute Love. I had felt her wonderful fragrance during our encounter.

I had observed how each chakra has its own quality. Open the door of the elevator and "welcome to a new world." Today, I compared it to tuning into the waves of a radio. Each radio wave has its own character and vibration, literally.

During the class break I asked Charles how to filter out all the sensations and impressions I was experiencing while channeling, because it was so much to process while I was trying to write. He said to do it ten times, then ask him. I felt as though I had a million questions for him . . .

By the time I had done it ten times I had already become comfortable with the experiences and received much assistance from guides who watched over me during the meditations. It was a quick learning curve.

Chapter 7

Lousiou

Later in the week I channeled another entity. Here is an excerpt.

I feel the joy in my heart as I begin to feel his presence. It makes me smile. I feel him looking down at me, in me, with benevolence.

"Tell me where you are from," I ask.

"I am from a place beyond your comprehension."

I must hold my attention and release my ego at the same time. As soon as I close my eyes I am greatly altered. I know that it is an exalted state that I feel. I feel very warm.

"What areas of knowledge do you share/communicate?" I feel a very high vibrational energy pattern in this guide. I feel him opening wide the top of my head. My eyes are fluttering. My gaze is upwards in my mind's eye. I feel joy and softness in my heart. Every time I close my eyes, I feel a great rush to the top of my head. Time to pause with writing and time to experience, I think to myself. Then I think to him, "You are teaching me to feel the great opening at the top of my head. You are a FACILITATOR. I feel myself in different places at the same time—me being HERE in my consciousness as well as being THERE." I recognize the being's individual density

in my body. I feel its lightness in my heart. Joy. He holds a commanding presence.

"It is with joy and delight that I assist an earnest being as you here today," he says. "It will be the beginning of a great adventure for you. Be earnest in your search. Continue your study. Events will come to you as you progress. Do not preoccupy with what's next. ALL IS TAKEN CARE OF. We are watching you. There is great joy in store for you. Much excitement and reward to come to you. Study and learn. ALL WILL BE DONE FOR YOU. Namaste to you". Lousiou is his name.

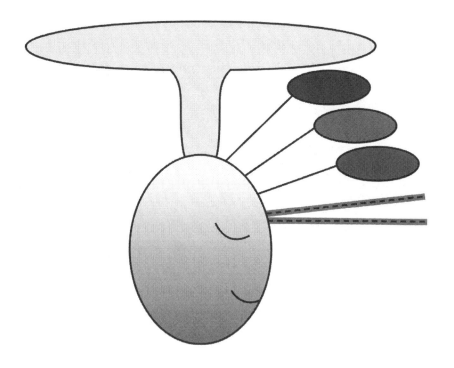

Secondary Chakras

I keep my focus on my crown chakra. I noticed it expand according to the size of the entity, as he left.

This is my lesson for tonight. Thank you. I have learned a lot tonight.

I close the top of my head and smile and my heart chakra feels extremely good. Calm, peaceful, and happy. My heart chakra feels filled with love. and great joy. I also seal the opening ABOVE my 3rd eye that is over my forehead. I have discovered during meditation several secondary chakras on my forehead, others that are between my third eye and crown chakra. Each is a portal to another realm.

I feel very altered. I have been meditating for 1 hr 15 minutes.

Thank you Guides and Masters for your teachings.

Blessings to you all! I exclaim.

Chapter 8

Your Gain Will Be Your Own Ascent

The following day I had another encounter during meditation. I grew respectful of those who are blessing me with their presence and teachings and was truly grateful for their visits.

I feel a man with heavy feet. He is well planted on the ground. His body is heavy. I feel a shift in consciousness as I try to follow his state of awareness.

I feel elevated to the ninth chakra.

I feel his body, face and mouth. "I know about many things, he says. I have extensive knowledge. I am heavy, Mongol – Oriental. I sit with only a loincloth. I weigh 265 pounds. I am here because I asked to be useful to the betterment of the universe. I want to contribute to its unfolding. We expect great things to come from this era of time. It is time to get back with Those [Higher Beings] who know of the workings of the universe. They [the workings] have been kept hidden for many centuries and millennium. I am here to teach you to access Those [from up on high] who have the old knowledge so that it may be made available again to the masses in this period of time. You must take care of your back. It is most uncomfortable, the pain there. Follow your truth. Be honest with yourself. You can ask to channel any time. The knowledge will be greater than your own current wisdom. Important things will be passed on to you. Your gain will be your own ascent. You have a pure nature that allows you to be an excellent empath, medium."

I didn't feel very comfortable in this chair and excused myself. "I'm so sorry again." Now I'm sitting on the bed. I asked the guides to help me find a meditation chair that will be proper for them during our sessions. I notice that I feel nauseous in my stomach as I also did last night after the session. "Thank you, I say, I honor your presence. I feel tired now and don't want to be disrespectful. I will not waste your time or impose on you by subjecting you to my lack of focus. I thank you again and look forward to the next time we will meet.

"Your student, with love."

Observation:

He was talking very fast. Fifty minutes had passed. I could see him talking, looking down at me. He was a no-nonsense kind of guy. He might have been the Meditator-For-Hire.

Chapter 9
Angels of the Higher Realms

On Sunday, November 21, 1999, I began my meditation. During this session, I noticed myself describing activities that I had never known possible, using words that were not part of my normal vocabulary to describe them. They just came naturally and I knew that they best described what I was experiencing.

You are an Angel. You entered me then turned to face me in my body. You have a white face, hair, robe.

What do I feel? I feel softness.

I say to him, "You are doing something to my light body. You are examining my light body. What are you doing to my light body?" [I was being given an attunement and balancing.]

"You are redesigning my polarities, adjusting my light body's polarities to make me more capable of functioning in this realm. How will it help me?"

"It will make you more lucid," I hear.

I see the angel change color. [He was white at first, then changed to red, then yellow.] Turning back to red now, he moved over to my right facing me. He is looking at my shoulder putting some green rays on it, to release the tension there. Now some blue there. He is equalizing my energy. [I was receiving a healing treatment. He was balancing my chakras.]

He is now working on the chakras in my head. He is working on the electrical brain patterns. I feel distorted – like a TV test pattern. I wait and allow him to do his work. I try to separate and not use my physical body to think (brain) – if that's possible . . . Now I feel a sensation in the area of my throat chakra as he moves his energy there also. I feel the energy he is using on me move downward. My head is becoming clear and the test pattern is gone.

I see the Angel turn yellow – yellow/orange now. I don't know what he is doing. He's still to my right.

I feel the top of my head activated. I think someone else wants to descend now. (2) He is old and large and in me.

He is a bald man. I see him sitting very comfortably. He has authority in his presence. (Thank you for being here, I think to him.) We hear distant church bells. He says: "What pretty music coming from the neighborhood church. I am happy that you have shown an interest in this sort of work. It is always something that rejoices us when we see one of you trying to contact us. Letting go requires some work, to be able to receive our messages. I am happy to help you with your efforts. Maintain your focus. Find my "signature" and hold on to it. Let go of your chakras. Good now. That's better. Do you like the place you see me from? Yes, you are above yourself."

He has turned around and is facing my body and I am above him, above my body in my light body. I don't want to interrupt him. He is probing me [making an assessment]. He is facing my light body now. I feel his presence. He says: "You will speak," referring to a concern I had about being able to vocalize their messages. Don't worry about it. You are doing it now. It is easy when you let go and simply feel ME. It is not so difficult, you see. Stop thinking so much. (He smiles) Allow yourself to see my thoughts as you do when you listen to other people's thoughts. You know how to do that. It is easy for you. Just listen to OUR thoughts. There . . . (I smile). Sweet one . . . it is nice to see you enjoy doing this. Glad to see your heart happy with the experience. Some things that you will experience through Us will have a serious tone (at times). This is important work."

I look at him from above. He is about 2 feet below me. I see the top of his bald head and his face. I try to connect to his energy. I have lost his "signature". He says: "There, you remember ME. Do I have to get inside your head for you to notice me? Stop doubting me. Remember the feeling. It's very real and unique to ME, and is pleasurable to you" [meaning that I enjoy his company]. I think to myself, why do I feel myself drifting? I feel some fear. He says: "There! I'm in your face again! (He makes me smile). Must I sustain YOUR focus? YOU are the one who is supposed to be helping us maintain our energy pattern on this plane. . . ." [When I channel beings, they each have an individual energetic signature, in the same way that we recognize people on Earth by a face or voice. The beings are foreigners, in a way, to the Earth plane's vibration. I tune in to their frequencies and use my focus to maintain the common line of communication. It is an exchange on a common frequency.] (Sorry) I feel compassion from his energy.

I say: "I'd like to get to know you better. I like you very much. How can I see you again? It would sadden me to never see you again. How do I ask for you again? You are so NEAT!"

He answers: "I will ask Those Above if I may work with you more. It was not intended but can be arranged".

I ask: "What should I call you? How do I refer to you"?

He answers; "You may call me Simon".

I say: "Get in my face again please. You are drifting away. Why are you so pensive?" He says: "There is a lot that you do not know. I say a special prayer for you".

He is serious now. He has moved to my left side as to send a message 'to the Others". He is busy communicating with them. I wait in anticipation . . . It takes a moment . . . Something is coming to me. I feel the left side of my brain and my left eye start fluttering . . . My 3rd Eye area is being activated. Something is being done to me . . . I wait for it to end. I take a deep breath. I feel something activated in my head. Working on my focusing ability . . . testing it. Adjusting my ability to sustain the activation. I feel as though I have been elevated. [Transformed would probably be a better word. I saw my light body receive a crystal treatment and my brain, throat chakra, and full body being activated, slowing my metabolism and heart. There was a change in my consciousness.] I don't know where I am. Something is happening.

There is someone else (3) in front of me. He is etheric, transparent, very large and carrying me somewhere. He is different. A Guide. Taking me somewhere. Keeping me close to him. I was asked if I wanted to go further a moment ago. I was afraid, but decided to go ahead. I took a deep breath. The Guide is comforting me. He is changing positions. He was facing towards the left before. Now we have stopped. He is standing towards the right and is standing in front of a portal. He is waiting for permission to enter. Everything is turning white in my head. They want to examine my "purity". They are also examining my heart chakra and I feel the etheric density in my head change. [This was the best way I could describe the sensation of examining the quality of my focus, the frequency of my thought patterns.] Now it has subsided and they have finished their examination. And I wait. Now I feel focused. The "atmosphere" is empty of color. Now I know that I am moving on to somewhere else. I am in ME and feel anticipation, of what, I am not consciously aware of. I apologize to them: "I'm sorry but my body is very uncomfortable and my legs hurt and I really need to go to the bathroom. But I don't want to lose the experience. I'll try to hold the focus . . .," as I get up to go relieve myself and come back to my chair.

I return and call my guide and he smiles. I notice that Simon is near my shoulder now. I am in good company! With the two of them with me, my energy is changing. I feel horny now. This Place where I am now is doing things to me. It is to my left. My Guide is facing to the left, looking upward to a beam of light that is coming down to us, as to take of the light energy coming from that direction. I am being inundated by it and allow my entire body to receive it. It is coming through the top of my head. I feel it in my arms and I try to hold this. This is great! I feel like a cotton ball. White, light, and fluffy (don't laugh). Like a fluffy cloud of cotton. Light in color but not bright white. I float and go to the left. What is all this for that I am doing this? Now I can't see my Guides anymore. I will call them. I feel that I hear them say: "Don't look with your eyes, only with your 3rd spiritual eye. Just feel and remember". (I hope I do). Wow! Thank you. It was worth going there. Thank you.

I never lose the awareness of myself when I am doing this. I smile and say: "Now what do we do next? (I love my Guide) This is great fun!"

Every time that I feel a slight anxiety I know that a wall is being broken down, and I am overcoming fear in my heart. It is a cleansing. I do not know where the blocks come from. I thank the Guides for challenging me to overcome them and get through it.

It is unusual to experience — now my throat chakra is being activated with heavy energy. It makes me cough. I wait . . . there is a pause . . . I sustain my focus . . . the "mood" is changing. There is a male entity, or maybe I feel a new Guide (4) that is present. A serious one. Very preoccupied with his work. I do not know what he is thinking. I wait. (I need more paper to write this and go get some. I'm back.) I look for my Guides again. Here is my friend (2) Simon. I see myself now IN my body. I had trouble being there for a moment and now it has passed. I see crystals in my light body!!! White. Scintillating! I thank the guides for spending time with me.

I feel altered again. I feel my brain cortex being activated now. I wait . . . I refuse to be tired now. I will continue. I am given resolve (strength to continue). I feel joy again . . . uplifting . . . makes me smile. I'm being "elevated". A lot of bodywork being done on me. Thank you. It is humbling. I feel elevated in my head. I am sustaining it. All those years of training, drawing has taught me to focus and discipline my mind for tedious and focused work. Where are my guides?? This is a long session.

I am channeling someone else (5) now. I recognize him as the one in Charles' blue chair the 1st time I tried to channel and my lips trembled when I was trying to speak. Who are you? I see him. I feel different. He is smooth and to my right. Feels like a smooth male energy. Pleasant. It is hard to describe. I'm trying to turn to see him to my right. I feel him there to my side. He feels all different from the others. He is doing something with his hands. They are positioned like someone playing the piano or typing. What is he doing! He does not talk to me. He is busy. He has settled in me now. He is sitting waiting to speak. He is serious now . . . Focused and solemn. He is slowing my metabolism and heart. He has a commanding presence. He is taller than me. About 7 feet tall, maybe . . . he is trying to speak. I'll try to get out of the way. He has a thin body, long face. I can feel his presence. I don't know if he will speak. There is something about the light in the room that is bothering him. Someone is guiding him. Now, there is a change in my consciousness.

I begin to think, "How long should I go on with this?" I think I should go back soon (end this). I have and am really enjoying this and would like to do it again. He tells me he is still with me. I give him permission to stay and ask him what he came for. He is not using words to communicate. That is why I could not hear him. He communicates with "no words" but WITH INTENT. I am trying to understand. He is saying to me (with words, I think): "All of my concerns (my worries about my current work situation, etc.) are unimportant (not to worry about). There is something greater happening right now that requires my attention. Just "maintain" the physical. Relax, relax. Do not burden yourself. You are being prepared for a mission. All this is a period of training. A lot of energy is being focused on you by Higher Guides/Beings who have you in interest. Continue your study. **Your physical ailments (rheumatoid arthritis) will be dealt with by us. You will receive a healing.** *We need you healthy to perform a special mission. You will be guided every step of the way. This will be very exciting for you . . . and enjoyable. Do not fear. Go forth with a happy heart. LUKE."*

I am back now. I feel refreshed. Not tired. I feel altered. And I look around the room. I will close my eyes and make "closure". I thank my personal guides for taking care of me throughout the session. I send a prayer of thanks to those who assisted me tonight. I thank them for their gifts. I feel altered. Outside my body. I don't feel my physical chakras at all. I feel lucid and objective.

I do not know what to say. I have nothing to say now. No thanks are required now. I just maintain this feeling.

132

This meditation lasted over two hours.

This encounter affected me profoundly. Many things were remarkable in this meditation: the number of beings encountered, the multi-dimensional quality of the encounters, entering another realm with the help of a guide, having to be given permission to access the realm, the examinations, new attunements and uses of color frequencies, overcoming fears, the renewed promise of physical healing for my rheumatoid arthritis and the purpose of the individual encounters.

I remember to this day, the fear I felt at times, not knowing what to expect, and the decision to trust and go on. I also remember the calm feeling when I returned. I was speechless. I had nothing to say. I just bathed in the exquisite peace.

I later realized that my encounters with the Higher Beings are a true gift. Every time they introduced me to a new realm, I would receive a new Attunement that harmonized me with the vibration of the realm. It allowed me to become familiar with the vibration so that I could later return and visit them on my own if I wished. I had never been aware that such beautiful realms of being and consciousness could exist. I would not have known how to recognize them, with my limited perception. I had to be taken there by my guides. Those encounters were Initiations.

Illustration: Attunements and Initiations

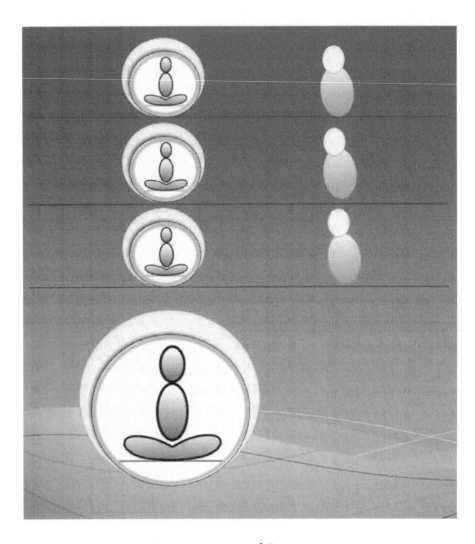

Attunements and Initiations

Chapter 10

Call Me by My Energy, Not My Name

I few days later, I begin another meditation.

I feel someone like "The Meditator-For-Hire" (higher?!!).

He is back. I recognize his "feel". He just told me I could request my past guides. He feels familiar to me, to my heart. He is objective and no nonsense. Not "gushy" and emotional/ warm. What should I call you?

*"**KNOW ME** BY MY ENERGY, NOT MY NAME."*

*"**CALL ME** BY MY ENERGY, NOT MY NAME."*

"THAT IS ALSO HOW YOU CALL THE OTHERS.

THEIR NAME IS SECONDARY."

"They know you by YOUR energy "signature". That is how they see you from the other realm. I see me as my energy. Recognize me as who I am – as a person sitting in front of you speaking, and just observe and listen. That is all there is to it."

"What can you tell me about my love life," I ask.

"(Ah,) Love . . . (he pauses). A lover is someone who teaches your heart to grow."

*I feel a magnetic connection into the Moment. I feel as though I am "sustained" in IT. The Meditator-For-Hire begins to speak: "Find that sustained feeling. Be deliberate. Seek it out. As Charles said, ask your guides to show you and teach you. They can show you better than he because they are **there** with you. It is a detached, uninvolved, nonemotional state of being . . . . Good! Now look for me . . . It is easier now. You can even see that page you are writing on with your Spiritual Eyes. See what you are writing. Your handwriting is becoming clearer, also your handwriting style is changing. Good . . . This is a class that we are having now. Listen closely and pay attention. You have been chosen for this job because you have the tenacity to follow through in the face of adversity. It is in your character/makeup. You have a deep spiritual conviction. We admire that quality in you. You must find a comfortable place to work. (I'm sorry, I don't have much $ to buy . . .) It will be provided for you. For now, slow down and practice. Practice channeling and writing. You cannot fly until you have learned to walk. Be patient. It will all be revealed to you soon enough."*

"There, you are doing well at sustaining your pattern at "neutral" like in an automobile. Now practice seeing with your Spirit Eyes. 3rd Eye. Look at the paper as you write. (I'm writing with my eyes closed all this time.) Hold the pattern in your 3rd Eye. It is easier. That is why it is called an "eye". It also has characteristic feelings associated with it. Keep breathing . . . become comfortable with it. Learn to

relax while you are doing it. Release all tension in your body. This does not have to be a tense activity. Practice and you will become more proficient."

Can we practice talking now. I ask?

"Yes. First let go of the crystal (that I have in my hand). It alters my energy . . . You need to stretch your ligaments. More oxygen in your body. Drink more water. Loosen your neck and shoulders. They hold a lot of tension. Maintain a healthy body—not just alive but VIBRANT with health. It will benefit you in receiving impressions. A vibrant body is a tuned antenna. Hold your questions. This is MY class. Do not interrupt. Thank you . . . Practice shifting into my energy pattern. Become familiar with it to the point of INSTANT recognition. Like a close family member." (I feel his presence in me. I feel his altered state and become aware of it. I stop writing now.) "You need deep work on your shoulders. EXERCISE. During meditation, try to see with your 3rd Eye and do things with your eyes closed."

I say goodbye. Thank him. He filled me with good vibes and left. Then we waited above me, (I was in my light body) and I RE-ENTERED back into my body. That is the orderly way to bring closure to a session.

Thank you for the class.

I was reminded again of his commanding presence as a Teacher. Very no-nonsense and to the point. I have learned much from him.

I have always been intuitive. Since my early teens I have experienced a wide range of psychic experiences. I had even considered at some point going to Duke University to be tested by some of their researchers in parapsychology. I had kept myself informed for years with the scientific studies that were conducted in the field. When I went to college, my main interest was to study the nature of time. I had experienced prophetic dreams for years and was curious to understand how it was possible to know of an event that was to occur in the future. Now, I began to notice that my intuition had been sharper and covering new areas that I previously hadn't had an affinity for.

In late November, I went to a powwow at Orange Springs, Florida. I met up with a couple of friends there, who were accompanied by others that I had not met before. I had brought my tarot cards with me and did five readings in a row for their friends. The readings were found to be extremely accurate by those who received them and there were comments such as, "That exactly describes the events that have happened to me in the last year," and, "You are the third person who had given me the same outcome," or, "That is exactly the way things are."

I felt there was a new fullness in the quality of the readings and a more well-rounded understanding coming from my connection to the Universal Source.

A few days later I met with a group to do some psychic exercises. Among the exercises, we practiced sensing impressions from objects with our intuition. I had never felt particularly successful in that area.

The first item was a button. I held it in my hand and received some imagery and impressions of a young preschool girl. I felt her personality as being stubborn and obstinate. The lady who brought the button said that it came from a plaid coat belonging to her aunt, who, she said, was "stubborn and obstinate!"

The second item was a silver bracelet. I felt that the woman who owned it was fat, small boned with small hands—a nice person who ate a lot of sweets. It turned out to be an exact description of someone's mother who owned the bracelet.

In early December, I began to realize that I was progressing (or ascending) to levels where it would become difficult for me to communicate or discuss my experiences with others. Someone who had not experienced these encounters may not be able to conceive of them. To explain them would sound like empty words to others' ears. There was a depth of understanding that could only be known through the heart.

Chapter 11

The Russian Warrior

In mid-December I had an interesting encounter during meditation.

I feel myself rising very quickly. I feel much love in me. It makes my heart smile. I feel PRESENCES all around. When I close my eyes I am immediately altered. I will keep them closed from now on no matter what as to not lose this feeling. I am speaking as I write to practice channeled speech. I asked my guides to be close to me as I open myself to loving beings from the other side. I wait for personal composure. I feel love and joy throughout, in a very mellow way (my mental state is mellow.) I feel my guides on each side of me and it feels very secure. I become mentally passive and receptive.

I feel someone descend in me. I feel his density and I feel altered. His heart muscle is heavier—larger—than mine. I remember to sustain his presence. He is Russian I think and wears a brown fur shirt and he is large, stocky and muscular. I ask him what he wants. What he has to say. He turned some time ago to look at me and he is facing me. His body is very strong and I can feel him touch me with his presence . . . I feel myself become warm . . . I am being energized. I feel hot. What is this for? It is to clear blockages in your physical body, he says. You need to clear your physical body and open the MERIDIAN PATHS within. (I tell myself that I need

141

to review these notes and follow directions.) My head is very energized by the presence of the Russian man. I think, is he leaving? No, he is standing to my right side now looking at me. Don't know what he is looking at in my Aura. He is giving me "milky" energy. I feel my spirit lifted to the "place of no words" [It is a place Charles takes us during meditation where we think without words, only intention.] . . . I also feel the milky energy rushing through my body and feel myself getting cold now. Is it the room or me? I will put on a shirt. I put on a sweater and am warm.

He is back in me. He has a large muscular chest, brown shirt and is fat. He is medium height. What do you want? He is a WARRIOR. He has a strong personality. I asked my guides if he is okay, am I safe with him? Now an angel has lifted me up far away and the density is gone. I feel clarity and lucidity. His intensity was more than I am normally accustomed to. He is nothing to be concerned about. I notice that my physical body and back hurt. I am out of shape. I move around a lot, feeling uncomfortable. I get comfortable and close my eyes.

Now I see a vision of early Russia and warriors, kings and soldiers. I see a scene of soldiers in a village, as though on a tapestry (I did a drawing) all displayed as if they are lined up for a battle. The villagers are just standing by the side of the road. I see a boy sitting on a window sill looking out at the scene. I see through someone else's memories, as though I am seeing the scene through someone else's eyes, perhaps the child in the window. I do not know where I am but I feel LIGHT (density). I see the village . . . I am floating, looking at it from above now.

He is back. What do you want? He is very dense and can be very forceful.

"*I have fought many wars and have won many battles. I am here to tell you that through all the wars and battles I have fought I have never heard a weak man [by that he meant a man who is in a position of weakness during a battle] give up when he had Faith. He has held his Faith as a beacon in times of turmoil. A man's Faith in his personal beliefs is not to be ridiculed. It is his sustenance and strength. He will endure countless abuses and in time he will be victorious if he holds on to his Faith, be what it may be. I am here with you today to tell you to remind people of their personal faith as it will carry them throughout their entire life. They are blessed by the Angels above for their strength and conviction! Love is bestowed to all of them. So be it.*"

I asked my guides to help me clear my body for re-entry. I am tired now and need to end this session at this late hour. My stomach is a little queasy. I am getting cold. Thank you for this session.

Later in the week, in class, I sensed that Charles was focusing a lot on me. I later realized that the guides had asked him to tell me something tonight. At one point he asked me, "What have you not accomplished yet? What do you think you need to do?"

I said that I did not know. He had me go up to my higher chakras and ask the question. I just felt a warm feeling in my heart. I said, "I guess I could just be nice to people, but that is not enough though."

He said, "If that was all that was required of you to do, would you be satisfied with that?"

"NO!"

He said, "Why not, are you not aware of the grandness of the Universe? What does your understanding of the Universe tell you?"

I told him that I knew that the universe was very big, very high, and goes very, very far. He said, "If God up on high wants you to just be nice, is that not enough? If God only requires that, should you question God's plan?"

I realized that it is silly of me to try to plan and control my purpose on this Earth. I felt thankful to Charles for conveying the wishes of those on the other side. They were watching and trying to keep me on track. I needed to get out of the way.

Chapter 12

Christmas Eve 1999

I did a special meditation requesting the presence of a high being who could speak a few words appropriate to this holy evening, on the eve of Christmas. This session lasted almost two hours.

I ask my Guides to put me in touch with a High Being that may convey a message tonight. I await their influence. I surrender to them and allow them to guide me. I feel slightly altered. I am following, being lifted to my higher chakras, very swiftly. I see and feel many angels' presence. They are soft and I smile with recognition. I feel their presence. "Thank you for this wonderful feeling." So soft, light, warm, trusting, loving and secure. "Take me with you."

We are in another realm. I am very lucid now. It is effortless to focus. I wait. I feel that someone is beginning to merge with me. I don't know if it is male or female. It is male but very soft and calm in nature. My mind is over analyzing and getting in the way. I will withdraw and observe. I feel and SEE through my feelings the beautiful feeling of an Angel. I feel very high and tall (I cannot explain, it is me and Him at the same time), I see from a different perspective, as if sitting on top of a high building, looking down. I sense a fullness of

KNOWING. What message do you have for me to dispense for you?

"It pleases me to see you do this work. It takes true dedication to try to reach us. It has been a long time since I have lived on Earth as a so called "light worker" as you would refer. The Earth is an interesting dimension with so many possibilities of expression. There are universalities (universal laws) that are found in all the realms. They are the Laws of the Universe. They make up its fabric, they are the weave of its structure. The laws are as real in their essence as the materials used in the construction of a house: the foundation of concrete, steel supports, walls to uphold the ceiling and roof, etc. To you, those materials are necessary for construction.

"However, the Reality of the Universe is much subtler.

"Before the Earth was created, there were other worlds and other realms and so on, and there will be others after the Earth is gone. Throughout all of time and infinity, there are laws that sustain the structure of this Grand Universe. Those laws are the foundation of all that is within it. They are Love first and from it, its expression. Truth, and the manifestation, the many realms of expression. It is so simple. Your realm of what YOU call duality appears complex to you because it holds so many possibilities, however it is very simple in essence. What is to be realized, and its true value and purpose is in its EXPRESSION of Love, and all that issues from it, many of which you already know.

These qualities are: reverence of a Supreme Essence, devotion to the Love, gentleness of heart, patience toward all forms of existence, appreciation of Truth, a desire to achieve perfection and sustain its Love, awareness of the Intelligence of the realm, a desire to sustain harmony.

It is possible for all forms of expression to rise to the highest of all realms because the Essence of the Universe is absolute and permeates all "so called" living things. No doors are beyond anyone.

All this of course is a vast subject to be covered at length at another time.

You have asked me to convey a message of Hope for this new age you are entering, a new millennium in Earth time. This is a symbol to people of this Earth as they enjoy giving themes to the passing of time, as they see it. I look at you all with great love. World occurrences may appear confusing to you. I ask all of you to raise your gaze to the Higher Values—the Great Values up on High. Those that have been carried down through the ages and have sustained civilizations, those values that trigger your Soul Memories. They are the truths of your heart and highest spirit. They are those that raise the highest part of your selves. Go forth with Peace. There is nothing to fear. You are Eternal. Love one another. You are never alone. You are forever showered IN the Light of the Highest Love." I thank him for his attention.

There is someone else. I ask, "What do you want to say? Who are you?" He is taking time settling in. He is adjusting to my brain, probing my head. Waiting. He feels like a bubble. I see him now. Have never seen anything like him. Don't know what it is but he is intelligent. He is light like a round bubble (it is difficult for me to put into words what is happening because I feel altered). What do you have to say to me on the advent of this millennium?

"It is an honorable man that has the desire to do what is of highest order. There is no relativity to the highest order. There is exactness to the Universe. It is self-sustaining. Whoever falls short of living in highest order is forgiven on Earth by the self-adjusting nature of this realm. People have forgotten their true nature. That is why so much Love is bestowed to them by the ones who watch them. I say to you:" "Rejoice in the Beauty and Intelligence of the Universe. Go forth and live the Highest Truths and Love one another. There is no higher purpose of existence on your plane."

"Thank you," I say. He is leaving now. I feel altered. There is a soft female presence in me. She is simple in demeanor and genuine in approach. She smiles. She is kind.

"What a wonderful night it is to be here with you. The love in the air is very inviting. It would facilitate the work of many Angels if people would open their hearts, as they are doing tonight. Why only wait for a special celebration to be open in their hearts with each other? This is a wonderful opportunity for all to show

much love. It is so simple yet people struggle so much. Love and the acceptance of Love open all doors. We are OVERWHELMED by the outpouring of Love, the collective energy of all of you this evening." [She was referring to all the people of the world who are celebrating this holy day.]

"Is there anything you would like to say to end your visit with me," I ask.

"I say to you, love one another close to your selves in Spirit. We are joyous and filled with the energy that you generate tonight as it goes forth through to us. You have our attention. We send Love to all of you." I thank her for her presence.

I thank my Guides as I come back . . . I feel very high. I am in another realm. I will close myself and see if I can sustain this feeling. Thank you for taking me there. I will re-enter my consciousness into my light body, and my physical body, and ground myself.

December 31, 1999

On this eve of a new year and new millennium, I pondered upon what I had learned and what I had to offer. The past few years had put me in touch with what was important. I discovered the richness of the world that surrounded me. Paraphrasing a quote by Henry David Thoreau, "I went to the woods to see what I could find, and know, when I die, that I had lived." I had learned that I need to show the Beauty that I love.

I prayed to those up on high, to show me the way. By their Grace, God's will be done.

Your will.

Not my will.

May God's will be done.

Chapter 13

January 2000 & Words of Comfort

Through the course of my duties at the cemetery, I had witnessed much love from families during their time of loss. The greatest beauty I had seen had been during funeral services. It was a time when people were truly genuine in their hearts. Their open and true expressions of grief were pure displays of love for the departed. I had often noticed that the deceased was present in spirit throughout the service.

I witnessed a particularly touching scene in January 2000 during the graveside memorial of a deceased military service man. It was a warm, sunny Florida morning. The attendees were standing under a shade tent, with the man's family sitting in the front row where chairs had been arranged. The American flag was draped over the casket and several military men and women were standing to the side of the assembly, preparing for their military salute. Then a bus arrived from the Veterans' Hospital. About seven patients in wheelchairs debarked from the bus, each with an attendee assisting them to the grassy area. They were friends of the departed. What surprised me the most was to see each of them also escorted with their own angel! We certainly were in good company! What a sight it was for me. Some had stories to share during the eulogy and there was so much love displayed on this day. It was a true gift to witness it.

Throughout January, I felt distressed because of tensions at work at the cemetery. Over the last few months, I had felt weary from a senior employee's constant lashing out at those who were within proximity. I tried to be kind and empathic, to overlook the behavior, but found it difficult not to be affected by it. I often asked the guides for help in dealing with this situation.

I was told in one instance:

> *"Hello Dear One. I am sorry to see you troubled. It is the nature of your realm that such difficulties will occur. I am sorry that it cannot be taken away from you. Such things are as they are. A growing being must be allowed to experience its opportunities for growth as it is expressed through their freedom of choice. It is a necessary part of their personal progress. You also are free to provide service and/or move on. Interactions between beings are very fascinating to us. It endears us to watch you grow. It teaches **us** that we are, as we are, by choice also. The Beauty of Experience is to experience God in its many manifestations (realms). I say to you Paula, make your own choices. Follow your path, show Love at every possible opportunity and uphold the Beauty of God. There is much freedom. Go forth. Take self-determination. The angels will direct you on to where you can do the most good. Be yourself and do not worry so much. It will become clear after you have moved on. The realm of*

the spirit ascends [gives you perspective on] your short-sighted view of these times."

I improved my meditation space and found a more comfortable chair.

During most of January, I received training from my Guides, experiencing other realms, developing my intuitive senses, and receiving attunements. There were several instances where I was told that plans were being made for me and that I would begin a new career.

Chapter 14

The Mischievous One, the Place

In January of this new year, I was initiated to a new realm and its special characteristic. I had been feeling restless and impatient lately.

I feel the area of my 3rd Eye being activated. I thank my guides and angels for being in my life and for allowing my awakening to occur. It is a wonder and a pleasure to be in their presence. Thank you for the understanding you give me. I feel the 3rd Eye area activating and feel a little altered. I will begin to focus and wait. There is someone. He is in me and wearing a white shirt. He is glowing in whiteness. I will stop thinking and feel with my heart. Who are you? He is adjusting being in me. He is moving in front of me, moving from side to side, doing something and looking at me. I am grounded in my body and stabilized by the being. He begins to speak.

"Hello. It is a pleasure to be in this form with you, together." He has a mischievous and devious (in a past life) personality. I ask him who he is, what his purpose is. "I am here to see that you are kept in good direction, that you do not wander into areas of detriment to you, because I am familiar with the unruly side of life. It is my salvation to do service with those who need direction." What should I do? "You must focus on

the Higher Values. I know that you want something of more earthly import. Be grounded. Do not fantasize. Maintain your focus ahead of you. You might miss something if you do not look at what is ahead of you. There is plenty of time for you. As Charles would say, "All can change in the twinkling of an eye." When we are ready for you to know more, it will be revealed as in the twinkling of an eye. Be at ease with what is happening. It is enough for you right now. Do you not have all you need? Enjoy the present and be grounded and focused and light in your heart. Do not be concerned with others' development. Do not be oppressed by THEIR experience of life. Each have their framework of understanding. Focus on your own. You are doing fine within your capabilities. Continue to learn. All is well dear one. Come with me and feel this beautiful WHITENESS that I carry." I am carried into the whiteness of his garment. I feel energy throughout my mind and body. I cannot think because I am very altered.

Now I see yellow in front of me. It is a rich yellow. I feel as though it has materiality about it. This is a PLACE. The yellow is a THING like a substance. Can I go up to it? Yes, if I don't think. No thinking in this place. Feel only. I smile in my heart. It is pleasant. I feel like a wave going through me. I focus my attention. They are waiting for me. What is this place? It is hard to formulate, to verbalize. I look for the one who brought me here. I feel his presence. I'm sorry my attention is wavering. I am preoccupied by other things (work). "Don't think so much! Allow yourself to feel . . ." he says. I'm getting hot. I'm very hot . . . I'm elevated. Shhhhhhh . . . My mind is heavy and sustained. I am sustaining a focus. It is the consciousness of THIS PLACE. "Maintain the focus. You finally understand," he says. "There is also an altered state of consciousness here. Your 3rd eye is focused here. Remember this place. It is a place to exercise your focus and develop dimensionality of consciousness. There, you remembered what to do here. Very good. You have learned much about the nature of the realm. Good, you are doing this well. It is fun. Yes, you become altered here. The more you are grounded and focus, the more you become altered at the same time." (It is as though I am aware of two experiences simultaneously.) "Do not daydream. Be CERTAIN! (grounded in reality). As you see, there is also a sensation in certainty. There is no need for wishful thinking. Here is a place for you to experience the feeling you long for. Yes, it requires concentration to maintain this altered state here. Remember this. There is much to be learned from other realms." What should I do now? "Relax and rest. Enjoy and learn." How do I come here again? "Ask a guide to show you again. Practice." I feel very high. I'm so stoned . . . When I don't think, I get really high. I am very high and cannot think . . . What do I feel? Not much emotionally. I'm just very high here . . . What is this place? I'm going to come back now. There doesn't have to be a purpose for a place like this. To just exist. It is enough in its beingness . . . Thank you.

I think of coming back and remember THE PLACE and feel high again. I take a deep breath. I'm going to come back now. I smile, and remember, and feel high. This is uncanny . . . I'm never going to get around to leaving! This is funny . . . Mmmmm . . . It feels so good. Who else knows about this place? . . . If I could bottle and sell it, I'd be rich! I don't mean to be disrespectful. You know if anyone is kidding. I feel this energy in my entire being. Don't forget to breathe, I tell myself. Gosh! This feels good in my head.

There were 2 beings that I encountered – the mischievous and devious (from a past life) and the one who took me to THE PLACE. Thank you both for this special treat. I'm very high and don't really want to open my eyes. I'm back and will sit here and enjoy the feeling for a moment. Thank you . . .

Can't think when I get that burst of HIGH. Hope I can do this again.

There were many blank spaces in my transcription because I could not read the words clearly. I am amazed to this day that I can write with my eyes closed and under extreme altered states of consciousness. My brain must be ambidextrous!

I found it interesting that one of my guides was providing service to atone for his past life on Earth. Yes, I was restless during these times and it was work for me to keep my discipline, faith, and composure. I was overly preoccupied with controlling my wants and desires and not seeing the gifts that were in front of me. But he stressed the importance of keeping on the straight and narrow by emphasizing the need to focus upon the higher values.

I continued attending my weekly classes with Charles and received wonderful teachings. Throughout the last year, I had diligently practiced meditations we had done in class. Now, I had begun to notice that the themes of my meditations and thoughts preceded those that would be presented in upcoming classes. These classes became a form of validation for me.

I began the Alliance of Divine Love's ministerial program at the Seraphim Center. It was a special accelerated course of the two year program that would end in April. I considered again whether I had enough time to take on the program, since the guides were preparing something special for me. I sensed that the course would end at about the same time that my new assignment would begin.

IV

Period of Waiting & Preparation

Chapter 1

Discipline & Practice

During this period of time, I practiced discipline: meditating regularly, receiving teachings from my higher beings on the state of my body and my chakras, maintaining focus in the presence of beings, and developing my awareness of subtle energy nuances. I was encouraged to carry a pure, loving heart, an appreciation of God's creations, and a humble reverence for the Divine. I received emotional support and encouragement that all would be provided for me and that my future was secure. Plans were being made where I would be able to provide service for the benefit of others and myself.

During this period of study of the Alliance of Divine Love ministerial course, I received further dimensional teachings (teachings from other Dimensions and beings) through dreams and was told that although I would not remember anything specific, I would notice in the future that I would "know certain things."

I realized one day that I had fuller and deeper insight into people's Higher Selves. Perhaps it had not occurred to me to look more deeply, and so I had not uncovered more aspects of it. Now, I could see their motivations, intentions and special talents before their birth on earth and could tell if they were expressing their true natures in life. I could also see which realm/world they had come from.

One day, I was doing a reading for a young man. I wondered, "Who is he?" So I looked at his Higher Self and went deeper. I then saw him as the spirit that he was before his birth. I saw his pure essence and the energy pattern that he projected. I saw his motivation as someone who scans his environment with great enthusiasm, taking on a broad view, with mature perspective and understanding. I understood that whatever he chose to give his attention to, he would apply this broad vision to.

I continued to follow his vital essence upward and could see his soul group, the soul family that he resonated with, like his home, and their realm. I could then follow him even higher to the part of him that was complete, beyond the desire for expression, the part that was one with the consciousness of the universe.

Surprised, I then viewed more people from that perspective and noticed that each person is unique in their essential quality and pattern of expression. I saw the worlds they originated from and realized that there were many, many worlds beyond our own. We are familiar with the angelic realm: however, there are many, many more.

Today, when I do a healing for someone, I first look at who they really are. Then I look to see how they are expressing their unique qualities. Many problems, —health and otherwise— occur when a person is not expressing his or her unique gifts and motivation. When beings take on human form, they have unlimited choices of what they can do. Their uniqueness is revealed in how they do it.

I received wonderful words of encouragement in February:

> *"Since you have begun communicating with us, you have grown a great deal. This is the course we have chosen for you. Your development will continue. There will be many beneficial (learning) encounters for you. You will be presented with many enlightening opportunities. It will be a pleasurable adventure. Trust us. We are watching you. You have many concerns about your earthly existence.* **Keep your gaze up to the heavens and your heart will follow.** *Concentrate on your growth. That is the essence of your joy. Feel your inner love and allow it to be expressed. This is your true light. Feel the inner love in your heart and express it at every opportunity. Encourage those kinds of encounters in your life and you will experience much contentment. It will feed from itself. You will benefit from such expressions and you will manifest the contentment and rewards you seek. It is not so difficult when you are in the flow. Do it! Be there in the flow and live radiantly. Keep your heart soft."*

I thought that the session was over, but then I was given the realization of a heightened sense of awareness, a fuller perspective, for this period of time I was living. I noticed that was capable of carrying much joy in my heart. I decided to let go of my worries and old patterns and embrace this awareness that I was being given.

It was easier than I thought.

In February I received many blessings. Materially, I was given an artwork commission, received money to repair my car, and taught a workshop at an art school in Lake City.

I received a teaching from a Guide on the nature of creativity and how we each play a part in creating the present moment:

> *"From this higher vantage point, I see creation as the direct effect of our will. It only reflects a response from our acts of creation. Everything we see is the outcome of our manifestations. **We are the ones turning the Wheels of Fortune.** Our actions originate from even higher realms! It all trickles down to where our consciousness is present (focused), through all the realms of life. We manifest on all levels at the same time. We are the Lords of our own Universes."*

In March, I continued to receive words of encouragement from my helpers. I received another prophetic message during meditation, of what was to come. Here is an excerpt:

> *"It has been some time since I have spent time with you. Let's take a few moments together and be together," the teacher says. Yes, my body is "out of sorts" these days, I said. It does not feel at its best. What do you recommend that I might not yet have considered or what would you suggest?*

"We suggest that you drink more water to flush out the toxins and open up channels of energy. As you might realize, it is important to be physically vibrant to better receive our impressions. However it is your choice, but you are receptive to the voice of common sense and reason. So, please give this consideration as it will benefit you on ALL levels. We might suggest that you plant a garden. It is good for the soul as well as the body."

I thank you for your suggestions, I say. I feel a malaise and uncertainty. What do you understand about this?

"You have been working hard and wonder if you will reap your just rewards. The Angel Gabriel (metaphorically) is thrashing down the obstacles that have been in your way and is facilitating the road of opportunity for you. Continue on your path. The doors will open up for you to pass through. There is no more time for you to be morose. This is a time for ACTION. "SEIZE THE DAY". You will be asked to express your SOUL. This is your time to share the Light of God and Love and Light. Be confident as we are by your side. NOTHING WILL BE BEYOND YOU (what you can manage). You are not alone. We ARE (with me in their beingness) and SURROUND you. Go forth with the joy and confidence that is in you."

Chapter 2

Reiki Session

I had my first Reiki session in March. The Seraphim Center had open sessions scheduled on Wednesday evenings and I had wanted to attend it to experience the healing energy. My friend Susan had recommended it to me.

I was rushing to arrive early and wanted to stop by the library on the way. As I hurried inside the library, I slipped on the steps, and sprained my ankle. I tried to ignore it and sat down to look up some reference material. When I rose up a few minutes later, I realized that my ankle was so painful that I had to skip and hop out of the building. A librarian came to assist me and wrote an incident report when she heard of the fall.

I told myself that this would be a good test for this healing modality. I hurried to the Seraphim Center and arrived near the end of the session. I hopped up the stairs in great pain to the second floor and entered a dimly lit room. There was a man lying on a massage table, and a man and a woman were working on him, giving him energy. They set a chair for me to sit by his feet. I was told to put my hands over his feet to catch the energy that they were going to send through him and that it would flow down his body into me. I could feel it in my hands. This lasted for some time. Then the two people left. The man on the table got up and began to work on me.

He worked on me for about one and a half hours. He checked my meridians and my chakras. He said that my stomach chakra was very dense and scratchy and my heart chakra was a little scratchy. I realized what he showed me. It was caused by stress. I had not been aware of it before.

Then he asked me to work on him. I told him that I had my own way of doing it and had not done the Reiki style before, but I also realized that what I did was similar energy work. He showed me how to work on the energy around the head chakra. I was very tired from focusing during the last one and a half hours of my session and did not know if I had the stamina to work on him, but did for another thirty minutes. It was as though I had gone to a class, and I learned much. I thanked him and left a donation for his time. I was surprised that the pain in my ankle had subsided by two-thirds!

I felt him send energy to my ankle every day around the same time of the day for the next week. Susan told me that he often did it as part of his meditation practice. I did not take any medicine: I put ice on it the first and second night and used an elastic bandage for two or three days. It healed remarkably quickly. He was an excellent teacher and healer.

I continued working on releasing stress and tension from my stomach chakra. "Letting go" was the theme for the following week during meditation— becoming more comfortable with my feelings, allowing myself to fully experience all sensations. Thanks to my spiritual healers, I saw the damage in my body, understood how it was caused, and how it manifested. I saw serious points of inflammation and focused on healing them. I was also encouraged to send Love to others.

On March 25th, I received another message about what was to come in the near future:

"Something that is going on around the 1st of April will show you the way to the path of your accomplishment. Go and be confident. Be in the present moment and do not fear the future. You are blessed with the spirit of God. All that is of true consequence is in the present. Be true and in Love. There . . . you can see the happiness in your heart. You see that your life is good to you. We will always be with you. Rejoice in the day."

Chapter 3
The Ascetic

The last week of March, I received a message in meditation from a Hindu ascetic who spoke about trust. Here is the excerpt:

I begin my meditation. I feel warm as the energy rises up my body, up the chakras. I am above myself now and wait for contact from the Guides. I feel the Love. I feel quite warm.

I sense a male energy and he has moved below me so I follow him to another astral plane (he is from a different vibration/frequency). I am beginning to feel altered there. He is thin, small boned, average to short in height for a man. He is almost timid, reserved in demeanor. I will attempt to make him feel more comfortable. I feel as though I am too strong for his vibration. I will have to help him. I send love. It feels good. I feel we are setting a bond between us. "I am your student," I say to him. "There is something you have to share. Please feel comfortable to speak." He is subtle and from a high realm.

He begins speaking:

"Detachment from all things. Some joys are for the living, some are for the eternal. The purpose of life is to experience the joys of God on earth. The beauty of our Lord God is manifest in all things. All of us are experiencing the dance

of the Lord. He and only He can create our destiny, as He is the All Knowing, all manifested and manifesting One and continues to provide life and love to all. Follow the examples of the Great Ones. Grasp your faith as an arrow and allow yourself to be carried by God's Plan. Maintain your resolve and live in the love of the Great One."

"I have a message for you from those who have been watching you. They would like me to convey a message to you regarding your upcoming change in career. Have faith in God. Through all your changes, He will set you on your path. There is no accident in the unfolding of events. It is meant to occur in a specific sequence of events. Enjoy the moment and allow the passing to occur naturally."

He is Hindu from India. He only wears a white loincloth. I hear him speak with an Indian accent. Humble in demeanor. Soft oily skin. A man 20-30 years of age. A priest or prayerful one.

I send him love and thank him for coming. He is not accustomed to speaking in this way through a medium. We are both learning, I say to him. He smiles in his light and thanks me in his intent, for the friendship. He feels relieved that this practice is over. What a beautiful soul.

I thank the guides for obliging me. I send them love and feel it from them also.

Chapter 4
Finally

On Thursday March 30th, I received a call from a colleague in the art community. He said, "I have a friend in Tennessee who is looking for a designer to work in his stained glass studio. He is well established and mainly focuses on new church projects and restoration of older windows. I mentioned you to him, and sent him a couple of sample photos of your drawings and paintings. His name is Mr.Gregg. I think you might want to speak to him."

How excited I was! Here was an opportunity to create meaningful work that would be inspiring and uplifting.

I called Mr. Gregg and he said, "I'd like to meet you ASAP. When can we get together?"

I made an appointment to meet him the following Monday. He gave me the address to his studio and said he would make arrangements at a nearby inn for Sunday night. How thrilled I was as I hung up the phone. I began to prepare for the twelve-hour drive north, perhaps leading to my new journey.

On Sunday, April 2, I left in the early morning. I said a few words to my guides, asking them to watch over me along the

175

way. The weather was cool and overcast, which made the driving easy on my eyes and the temperature comfortable. It being Sunday, there was little traffic and I enjoyed the first few hours gazing at the countryside and rural farmland of South Georgia. I stopped for a short break and coffee and reviewed the driving directions on my map. It would be another three hours before I reached Atlanta, then I would be headed toward the mountains.

I continued driving north, and as I arrived near the outskirts of Atlanta, the sky began to fill with menacing, dark clouds. The number of cars on the road had increased, and now I was in the midst of heavy traffic. Yet it did not slow down the pace of the cars, as they seemed to move even faster. I kept up with the flow of the traffic, reading the direction signs by the side of the road. As I reached Atlanta it began to rain. Dark storm clouds were releasing their dense shower of rain, and thunder and lightning were all around. I maintained my eyes on the cars ahead of me while trying to read the direction signs. Then the rain became even heavier, and I could not see any cars around me or even locate the side of the road. I felt afraid and wished I could simply stop and park until the storm subsided. All I could see in front of me was a white sheet of rain pounding down on my car.

I began to follow a pair of red taillights from the vehicle ahead of me. I did not know where it was headed, but I had no choice other than to follow it. I was driving blind as I struggled to keep up with its rapid pace. The sounds of the rain and thunder were unnerving, and I knew that straying from my beacon of red lights would mean immediate collision with my surroundings.

As I have often done in unfamiliar places, I continued to follow the lights, hoping we were all headed to the same destination. After what seemed like a much-too-long time, the rain began to lighten, and I could finally see that I had been following a commercial truck. I was now able to make out the interstate signs and realized that we had driven through the densest part of Atlanta and were headed northbound out of town. Phew! It was undoubtedly the most frightening moment I have ever experienced on the road.

I passed many accidents on the road. Emergency vehicles were attending to the injured people and damaged vehicles. I felt as though my guardians had protected me the whole way. As soon as I was finally out of the city I stopped by a rest area to step out of the car and breathe.

I continued driving for the next few hours. At one moment I screamed "Yeah!" without consciously knowing why, until I saw a road sign saying "Tennessee".

I finally arrived in Nashville and directly headed to the glass studio. I located the street and recognized the building with my heart. I felt it immediately. I drove down the block and returned. I parked the car in front, took out my umbrella and walked up closer. I gazed inside the studio and read a sign, "Mr. Gregg." I saw the glasswork displayed in the window and knew I was home.

A message from Mr. Gregg awaited me at the inn when I checked in. He welcomed me and was looking forward to our meeting the following day.

The next morning I promptly returned to the studio at nine a.m. for our meeting. Mr. Gregg was a tall, burly man with dark hair. He had a soft voice, warm smile, and gentle demeanor. He walked with an easy shuffle as he led me to his office. On the walls were watercolor sketches of church windows, a poster of Tiffany glass from a museum, photos of his family, and architectural renderings of past projects. We sat at his desk, and I laid out my portfolio of drawings and paintings. As he looked over them, he began to speak to me.

"My daughter has been designing windows for me for years but now she just graduated from college, got married, and moved away. I'm going to be replacing her in the company."

We talked for a long time. He asked me when I would be available to begin because he needed someone as soon as possible. I told him that I could move at the end of the month. I had a couple of things to take care of. (I didn't mention that my ministerial ordination was in ten days.)

We went out to lunch, accompanied by his studio manager and his head artist. We chatted for a while and I could tell that this was an opportunity to meet some of the other members of the company. We ended our conversation with him saying that he would call me in a couple of days after he had spoken with his managers. I left feeling that this man had a good heart and would be good to work with.

I got in my car and headed back on the road for the twelve-hour drive home. It was still raining, and I arrived in the early morning hours of the next day.

Two days later he called me and made me an offer to work at his studio. He also offered to pay the cost of my move there. I was so thrilled, and I accepted.

That night I thanked those who were with me during my drive to Tennessee for their close guidance. As I meditated, someone came and sent me a vision:

First I saw a church in the downtown area with a steeple. A grey stone church. I noted that there was something or someone there for me. I sensed it was where I was moving to. I discovered later that it was St. Paul Catholic Church, over 100 years old. I went to see it one Saturday night. Yes, it was kept unlocked, even in these days of crime. It had Tiffany-style windows, with the religious figures beautifully painted. The glass was exquisitely manufactured by hand in the traditional way. I was preparing to design an additional window for the church and wanted to sense the flavor of the space. I pushed the front door and it opened. I walked in and it was dark except for a small light by the altar. So I turned on several lights and saw the beautiful windows that proudly stood along the walls. It was a small church, like they used to build in small communities. I sat quietly and absorbed the feeling of this place. I closed my eyes and felt the Beings that occupied the space. They had been here for a very long time. This was their space. I silently told them that I was here to meet them, that I was preparing to design a new commissioned window that would represent the Archangel Gabriel casting the devil out of heaven. I told them that my intention was to design a window that would please them and respect the history of this space. I asked for their guidance throughout the design process and manufacture of the new window. They appreciated the respect given to them in planning this new addition.

Then I heard my guide say:

"Come with me and I will take you to a place of Love, peace and joy, into the hills of your youth. A place where you grew up and began your beginnings/transformation/growth. A familiar place from your past. Many memories are there. You will feel them in your heart. Honor the past. It is the foundation of your beliefs.

Who are you?

"I am Regent. I direct people to their SOUL purpose. I bring out the hidden motivations. (He is close to Earth manifestation.) Follow your dream/destiny. Be true to your yearnings." (I have a past life memory in Tennessee.)

I learned that there are many plans, on many levels. There are many experiences to be learned simultaneously in one environment.

I visited my rheumatologist for the last time before my departure to Tennessee. She remarked how I had greatly improved over the last couple of years and recommended that I might consider ending my treatment for rheumatoid arthritis. I was in remission. I continued to improve and the condition has never returned.

Conclusion

In the years that followed, I was given the support and guidance I needed to perform my work. Soon after moving to my new apartment, on the full moon of Wesak, I was sitting in silence feeling alone in this new city. I closed my eyes in reverence of this special day.

I began meditating and was immediately approached by several High Beings, joyful as children. They announced that they were going to show me something that would allow me to grow and give me new insight. It would be a new realm. Then I saw others coming toward us from above, as from a hill ahead of me. There was a yellow light coming down and I felt joyous excitement in the air. "What do you want to show me?" I said. I felt purple light in my heart chakra and it was balanced. "You will understand a new depth in your heart," I heard. Something that cannot be learned through your realm of experience. It is a BAPTISM." I felt peace in my heart. Calm. I saw the amethyst-like purple color, dark purple. Then someone was here, I sensed his role was as a spiritual leader.

*I felt myself being carried above the beings, as though in a victory celebration, into a yellow realm. I felt embarrassed, because **they** are those I look up to. What is this celebration? "Feel this place dear one, this is your Home. In your heart of hearts, your brothers and sisters are here. All those who have known you since the beginning of time. There are other realms beyond where there is no identity* *(personal) and we all originated from it. But here, we each are as kin. You are Home. Praise God's Love for all of eternity. Sing the joy of his creation and existence. Praise the Great Plan as it is perfect and whole. Words cannot convey this meaning. However there is much more that can be felt through the heart of your highest soul. Peace be forever with you sweet one. Welcome!"*

I looked into this realm and its light was so bright that I could not distinguish all the souls that dwell in it. It radiated great vitality. It is intelligence beyond words and understanding. It is a knowing. I knew there would be an unbroken thread linking me to the realm from now on.

I often returned to this realm filled with so many bright souls, blending into its billions of lights, resonating at a high frequency of joy and pure energy.

In the following months, I was taken to other realms where there are schools of higher learning. One was a city made of crystal structures, where I received an initiation on the power of colors, for use in art and healing. I also visited realms of pure consciousness, where souls experience each other through pure presence. I saw life created before my eyes. I experienced the presence of Higher Beings, so vast in their Wisdom, Love, and power, that I would have kissed their feet, as if they were gods. That is when I realized that the Divine essence is so great, endless, and eternal. Where I once believed in a personal God, now I experienced the Divine as a universal presence that fills me with exaltation and peace.

How do I end this book?

I am a changed person from the one at the start of the book. Now, my perspective has deepened. I continue to be in awe of the glory of life. The universe is infinite. There will always be more to learn, more to discover. Yet I know now that I don't *need* to know everything. What I know is that the Divine essence is right here inside me. It is the life force, the creative expression embodied in me. It is as close as my Self, and it is all that exists and has ever been. It is also the pregnant pause. I have come to realize that my spiritual teacher, the Meditator-for-Hire was actually a meditator for Higher!

Someone asked me, "What do you do now? Would you want to sit, meditate and explore the vastness of the universe?"

I answered, "I am here, now. All there is left for me to do is to simply go, and live life."

It might seem mundane, but is it not why we are here?

Made in the USA
Middletown, DE
15 September 2018